ST. MARY'S COLL
ST. MARY   SO-AJE-557

THE LIBRARY
ST. MARY'S COLLEGE OF MARYLAND
ST. MARY'S CITY, MARYLAND 20686

LINCOLN AND THE POETS

LINCOLN
and the Poets

*

An Anthology Edited and with a Commentary by

William W. Betts, Jr.

UNIVERSITY OF PITTSBURGH PRESS

Copyright © 1965 University of Pittsburgh Press
Library of Congress Catalog Card Number 65–16455

Manufactured in the United States of America

28207

to JANE *and* MICHAEL

Preface

THE assassination of Abraham Lincoln on April 14, 1865, brought forth at once hundreds of Lincoln poems, most of them emotional elegies, some of them simply belated tributes to a President whose greatness had for so long gone unacknowledged. In the one hundred years since that tragic event we have had from our poets, besides those lyrics occasioned immediately by the fact of the assassination, countless additional tributes to the figure and the saga of Abraham Lincoln. Probably no other single episode in the history of the United States has been so often the poet's inspiration.

Naturally even the name of Abraham Lincoln has not been sufficient to protect most of these poems against the ravages of time. Of the thousands of Lincoln elegies probably no more than fifty genuinely dignify their subject, and of these only a very few attain to the highest level of poetry. But these poems taken together provide the most fitting, as well as the most enduring, memorial to the President.

Typical of the kind of lyric that has been swallowed up by time is the elegy appearing in a *Punch* memorial to Lincoln. The poem is by Tom Taylor, the prolific English dramatist who had written *Our American Cousin,* the play which Lincoln was watching the night he was shot. Entitled "Abraham Lincoln, Foully Assassinated, April 14, 1865," it was received with enthusiasm by its earliest readers. By Andrew Boyd of New York it was regarded as "magnificent." Boyd printed and distributed as a broadside, together with his own approbations, two of the poem's nineteen stanzas:

You lay a wreath on murdered Lincoln's bier,
*   You, who with mocking pencil wont to trace,*
Broad for the self-complacent British sneer,
*   His length of shambling limb, his furrowed face,*

.   .   .   .   .   .

Yes: he had lived to shame me from my sneer,
*   To lame my pencil, and confute my pen:—*
To make me own this man of princes peer,
*   This rail-splitter a true-born king of men.*

Clearly, though the sentiment here may be deeply felt, Tom Taylor's eulogy, especially if these are the two best stanzas, is not the kind of lyric that readers one hundred years removed from the occasion would call magnificent. And over the years there have appeared scores of such elegies. Among the distinguished and semi-distinguished American writers who have produced Lincoln-lyrics not likely to survive, to mention but a few, are Bayard Taylor, George Henry Boker, John James Piatt, Julia Ward Howe, Witter Bynner, Maurice Thompson, Edmund Vance Cooke, Charles Leonard Moore, Walter Malone, Martha Keller, Samuel Valentine Cole, Eleazar Parmly, "Neal Neff," Martha Parks, Florence Pratt, Frank Moore, Rose Terry Cooke, Henry Brownell, Joel Benton, Richard Watson Gilder, and John Kendrick Bangs.

Some seventeen years after the murder of the President, Osborn H. Oldroyd, the energetic Lincoln collector and biographer, addressed to some of the most conspicuous men in the public life of the United States and Europe requests for Lincoln testimonials. Sometimes a memorable poem is induced in this way. Milton's "Lycidas" is an instance. But great poems are rarely to be discovered among those that have been solicited. Unless a genuine poet is already on terms with his subject in spirit no immortal poem will emerge from such a request. Certainly the poet laureate, whose job it is to put the sentiment of the country into exalted rime, does seldom produce a truly memorable occasional poem, perhaps indeed because it is his job so to do. Public feeling is one thing, and private feeling is another. In any case, Longfellow seemed to appreciate the difficulty. He responded to Oldroyd from Cambridge on March 13, 1882: "Unable to do more than wish the undertaking great success."

Perhaps because of his advanced age (he was then seventy-five, and would die within a fortnight), the People's Poet could never have produced the poem. But it is likely had he been called upon by the Muse as well, rather than by Osborn Oldroyd only, he would have proved most royally.

When Oldroyd in 1915, the fiftieth anniversary of the assassination, had printed in Washington, D. C. his collection of Lincoln poems (he had selected eighty-nine), those which were notable were those which had already been at hand.

Some of these elegies, and some others produced by American poets in memory of Lincoln, have survived a significant test of time, and certainly it is fitting that on the centennial of the assassination these should be assembled. Naturally the lyrics which appear here are unequal in poetic merit. And naturally, too, not all readers today will agree on which best express the proper feeling for Lincoln. Some will prefer Whitman's Lilacs poem to all others; some will think the lyric by Edwin Markham the noblest of them all; some will acclaim the elegy by John Gould Fletcher, or "The Master," by Edwin Arlington Robinson; still others will respond most immediately to "Abraham Lincoln Walks at Midnight."

But most of the poems printed here belong to the first

rank of poetry. They are a credit to Lincoln and to the American poetry. Those few lyrics that do not attain to the highest level have endured either because they have been conceived by a poet of distinction or because they make a unique contribution to the total impression of the martyred President.

The writer is grateful to the Research Council of Indiana State College for a grant in support of publication, and to the librarians and staff of the Rhodes R. Stabley Library at Indiana State College for many courtesies and kindnesses, especially those extended in procuring inter-library loans. Grateful acknowledgment is also made to the following copyright holders for permission to reprint copyright material:

To Appleton-Century—for "Nancy Hanks, Mother of Abraham Lincoln," from *Going to the Stars*, by Vachel Lindsay. Copyright 1926 by D. Appleton and Company; copyright renewed, 1954, by Elizabeth C. Lindsay.

Mrs. Olive H. Barbour, Miss Ellen W. Dunbar, and Mrs. Anna D. Partridge—for "Lincoln's Dream," by Ridgely Torrence.

Brandt & Brandt—for "Nancy Hanks" and "Abraham Lincoln," from *A Book of Americans* by Rosemary and Stephen Vincent Benét (Holt, Rinehart and Winston), copyright 1933, 1961 by Rosemary Carr Benét.

Brandt & Brandt—for a passage from *John Brown's Body* from *Selected Works of Stephen Vincent Benét* (Holt, Rinehart and Winston), copyright 1927, 1928 by Stephen Vincent Benét, renewed (1955) by Rosemary Carr Benét.

Dodd, Mead & Company—for "Lincoln," by John Gould Fletcher.

Mrs. Marguerite Foster Fetcher—for "Lincoln" and "Nancy Hanks," by Harriet Monroe.

Harcourt, Brace and World, Inc.—for "The Long Shadow of Lincoln" and a passage from *The People, Yes*, by Carl Sandburg.

Holt, Rinehart and Winston—for "Lincoln," by John Gould Fletcher.

Houghton Mifflin Company—for "The Dead President," by Edward Rowland Sill.

The Macmillan Company—for "Babylon, Babylon, Babylon the Great," "Abraham Lincoln Walks at Midnight," and a passage from *Litany of the Heroes*, by Vachel Lindsay.

Virgil Markham—for "Lincoln, the Man of the People," by Edwin Markham.

Mrs. Ellen C. Masters—for "Anne Rutledge," "William H. Herndon," and "Hannah Armstrong" from *Spoon River Anthology*, by Edgar Lee Masters (Macmillan, 1914, 1942).

Charles Olson—for a passage from "Anecdotes of the Late War," from *The Distances*, by Charles Olson (Grove Press, 1960).

Arthur B. Spingarn—for "Memories of Whitman and Lincoln" from *The Sea*, by James Oppenheim.

"The Master" is reprinted with the permission of Charles Scribner's Sons from *The Town Down the River*, by Edwin Arlington Robinson. Copyright 1910 Charles Scribner's Sons; renewal copyright 1938 by Ruth Nivison.

Table of Contents

And when he fell in whirlwind, he went down
As when a lordly cedar, green with boughs,
Goes down with a great shout upon the hills,
And leaves a lonesome place against the sky.
—EDWIN MARKHAM

Introduction

ABRAHAM LINCOLN loved poetry. We know that he read with excitement the English Shakespeare, Burns, Byron, and Thomas Hood. We know that he was enthusiastic about a number of American poets, especially Oliver Wendell Holmes (his delight in "The Last Leaf" is a familiar story), James Russell Lowell, and William Cullen Bryant. Longfellow is supposed to have moved him to tears and it has been testified that he was among the first in this country to enjoy *Leaves of Grass*. One of our greatest regrets about Lincoln is that he could not in a well-deserved rest from the White House return to the poets he loved.

And the poets' affection for Lincoln was large. In the troubled times preceding and during the War Between the States, the American poets, notably Longfellow, Lowell, and Bryant, were among the first in the country really to appreciate the greatness of Lincoln as man and as President. While he lived he was for them the Great Emancipator; after his death he was the Martyr-Chief, My Captain, The Master, and The Man of the People.

Among the poets of Lincoln's time, some, especially William Cullen Bryant, knew Lincoln personally. Others, like Walt Whitman, though they never met the President, were in position to study him closely in the war city of Washington. Some, like Ralph Waldo Emerson and Longfellow, wrote of him from a greater distance. But whatever their association all spoke at once or eventually with affection and regard for the President. In his famous essay-analysis of Lincoln Emerson observed that in his conduct of the war he was "no holiday magistrate, no fair-weather sailor. . . . He is the true history of the American people in his time. Step by step he walked before them; slow with their slowness, quickening his march by theirs, the true representative of this continent; an entirely public man; father of his country." And Longfellow, whose oldest boy, Carl Sandburg tells us, "was shot through both shoulders with a rifle ball in the last battle of the Rapidan" and "came home suffering from the great wound," was, chiefly because of Lincoln's attitude toward slavery, early full of praise for the President. In a letter from Cambridge, dated on Washington's birthday, 1881, Longfellow thanks his friend Isaac Arnold for his sketch of the Lincoln-Douglas debates:

I have read it with interest and pleasure, particularly the part of it which relates to Mr. Lincoln. I well remember the impression made upon me by his speeches in his famous political canvass, in 1858, as reported in the papers at the time, and am glad to find it renewed and confirmed by your vivid sketches.[1]

Longfellow, like Whittier and Lowell, was enthusiastic in the cause of Abolition. A close friend to Charles Sumner, he had already written a number of anti-slavery poems, and it is not surprising to find him confiding to his diary on New Year's Day, 1863: "A great day. The President's Proclamation for Emancipation of Slaves in the rebel States goes into effect. A beautiful day, full of sunshine, ending in a tranquil moonlight night. May it be symbolical." [2] Of course Longfellow had already made the physical Lincoln into a symbol,

---

[1] Quoted by James Harkness and R. Gerald McMurtry in *Lincoln's Favorite Poets* (Knoxville: University of Tennessee Press, 1959), p. 55. See Harkness and McMurtry for details of Lincoln's interest in Longfellow, as well as other poets of his time.

[2] Quoted by Harkness and McMurtry, p. 56; also by Carl Sandburg in *The Prairie Years and The War Years* (New York: Harcourt, Brace and Co., 1954), p. 347.

writing: "He stands six feet two in his stockings—a colossus holding his burning heart in his hand to light up the sea of life." And as additional evidence of the great esteem in which he held his President there occurs in his journal for November 10, 1864, this entry: "Lincoln reelected beyond a doubt. We breathe freer. The country will be saved."

The poet's great concern that the Union be preserved is clearly the inspiration for his lyric "The Building of the Ship." The famous last stanza, especially when recited movingly by such readers as Noah Brooks and Fanny Kemble, is supposed to have won hundreds to the Union cause:

> *Thou, too, sail on, O Ship of State!*
> *Sail on, O UNION, strong and great!*
> *Humanity with all its fears,*
> *With all the hopes of future years,*
> *Is hanging breathless on thy fate!*
> *We know what Master laid thy keel,*
> *What Workmen wrought thy ribs of steel,*
> *Who made each mast, and sail, and rope,*
> *What anvils rang, what hammers beat,*
> *In what a forge and what a heat*
> *Were shaped the anchors of thy hope!*
> *Fear not each sudden sound and shock,*
> *'T is of the wave and not the rock;*
> *'T is but the flapping of the sail,*
> *And not a rent made by the gale!*
> *In spite of rock and tempest's roar,*
> *In spite of false lights on the shore,*
> *Sail on, nor fear to breast the sea!*
> *Our hearts, our hopes, are all with thee,*
> *Our hearts, our hopes, our prayers, our tears,*
> *Our faith triumphant o'er our fears,*
> *Are all with thee,—are all with thee!*

The President himself was much excited by the poem. On the occasion of its recitation before him he is supposed to have remarked gravely, "It is a wonderful gift to be able to stir men like that."

Longfellow very nearly met with Lincoln in the signal moment of the President's life. Along with Bryant and Lowell and George Boker, he had been asked to write a dedicatory ode for the services establishing a National Cemetery at Gettysburg. The ode was to be set to music and sung by the Baltimore Glee Club. Thus, had he accepted, he would have been seated on stage next to the President. But not Longfellow, nor any of the others, for one reason or another, felt he could supply the poem.[3] Perhaps all sensed intuitively that the President himself would that day be the Poet of Gettysburg.

Among the later American poets, who could never have known Lincoln personally or had any firsthand relationship with him, are a number who are nevertheless in another way as close to him as were the poets of his time. Carl Sandburg, Vachel Lindsay, and Edgar Lee Masters all were reared in the Lincoln country of Illinois, in an atmosphere electric with Lincoln lore, while E. A. Robinson, Stephen Vincent Benét, and John Gould Fletcher industriously became richly informed students of the historical Lincoln.

These poets, old and new, have quietly molded the figure of Abraham Lincoln into an impressive symbol of the nation's ideals.

It was Walt Whitman who observed that the "United States themselves are essentially the greatest poem." The Good Gray Poet was among the first, too, to recognize that in the figure of her sixteenth president, there was best represented the United States and all the new country stood for:

[3] See Harkness and McMurtry, p. 56.

Pictures of growing spring and farms and homes,
With the Fourth-month eve at sundown, and the gray
   smoke lucid and bright,
With floods of the yellow gold of the gorgeous, indolent,
   sinking sun, burning, expanding the air,
With the fresh sweet herbage under foot, and the pale
   green leaves of the trees prolific,
In the distance the flowing glaze, the breast of the river,
   with a wind-dapple here and there,
With ranging hills on the banks, with many a line against
   the sky, and shadows,
And the city at hand, with dwellings so dense, and stacks
   of chimneys,
And all the scenes of life and the workshops, and the
   workmen homeward returning.

In his death by assassination on Good Friday of April
1865, Abraham Lincoln achieved an immortality among
not only the people of the country he had led through the
terrible war, but among people of the world everywhere
who respect the principles of love and brotherhood. But
especially for Americans he symbolized the ambition to
realize a dream of peace and plenty, an America teeming
alike with bounty and privileges, an America of energy and
vision.

From the hour of the President's death, when Walt
Whitman conceived the impressions that were to take form
in the beautiful elegy "When Lilacs Last in the Dooryard
Bloom'd," through the first World War and such poems as
Vachel Lindsay's "Abraham Lincoln Walks at Midnight"
and John Gould Fletcher's "Lincoln," until Stephen Vin-
cent Benét and the present day, the figure of Abraham
Lincoln has been an inspiration to the poet.

Reflecting as they do the diverse personalities of the
many poets, the lyrics themselves are in many tones: the

somberly meditative reflection on his death, the exultant tribute to his stature as man and statesman, the bitterly indignant, and the quietly ironic. But all are alike in expressing an uncommon respect for an uncommon common man. And many, like Whitman's "Lilacs" and E. A. Robinson's "The Master," are among the most imperishable poems of the American literature.

LINCOLN AND THE POETS

William Cullen Bryant

1794–1878

AMERICA's first real poet, William Cullen Bryant, who as a boy of sixteen had begun the somber reflection on death, "Thanatopsis," was seventy years of age at the time of the assassination. But he had known Lincoln for a number of years and they had felt a mutual regard for each other. One popular story has it that Lincoln had once said of one meeting with Bryant: "It was worth the journey to the East to see such a man."

Their first meeting occurred in 1842, when Lincoln as a young military officer was serving in the Black Hawk War. Bryant reported later that he was "much impressed with the captain's good sense, well-chosen diction, and keen wit, to say nothing of the fact that the fellow's numerous early anecdotes were never pointless." [4]

He didn't know at the time, of course, but Bryant was to see a good deal more of that remarkable young man. He met him, in fact, just five years later, in Chicago at the River and Harbor Convention.

But the most important meeting for both occurred in 1860. Lincoln had just emerged triumphantly from the series of debates with Senator Stephen Douglas, and was actively seeking the Republican nomination for President, when on February 25 he arrived in New York City for the first time. On Monday the 27th he was to address what Hor-

[4] Harry Houston Peckham, *Gotham Yankee* (New York: Vantage Press, 1950), p. 105.

1

ace Greeley's *Tribune* would label next morning "as large an assemblage of . . . intellect and culture as America's greatest city had ever known."

The meeting was held at Peter Cooper's Institute (the largest auditorium in the city, seating over 2000 people) and chairman for the evening was William Cullen Bryant, then editor of the New York *Evening Post* and a conspicuous figure (at sixty-six) in the Young Men's Central Republican Union. Only about 1500 of the seats were taken (at 25¢ admission) because of a heavy snowstorm; but the audience from the first, in response to Bryant's introduction, was enthusiastic.

Carl Sandburg in *The Prairie Years* reports that Bryant "told the audience of Lincoln's majority for the senatorship in Illinois and the legislative apportionment that elected Douglas." The editor's closing remarks, Sandburg tells us, were received with loud cheering: "I have only, my friends, to pronounce the name of Abraham Lincoln of Illinois, to secure your profoundest attention."

With this introduction the clean-shaven Lincoln, who "towered a good eight inches above the polished metropolitan editor," went on to speak in his high-pitched voice with "eloquence, moral earnestness, even dignity." [5]

Bryant had for a long time been very fond of William H. Seward of New York, whom most people were expecting to win the Republican nomination, but the young lawyer's address on this evening and the sustained applause that it excited were impressive to him. Next day his paper printed in full the candidate's text and Bryant accompanied this with an editorial ringing with praise for Abraham Lincoln.

From that night on Bryant labored through editorials and liberal newspaper space for Lincoln to secure the election for his favorite. In the early years of the Civil War, however, the poet's enthusiasm for Lincoln fell off sharply.

[5] Peckham, p. 145.

Apparently he misunderstood the President's relationship to the Cabinet, the Congressional leaders, and the military staff. He feared from time to time that he had helped elect, in the most critical time, a weak and confused man. Early setbacks to the Union forces inspired Bryant to write to John M. Forbes: "I am so disgusted with Lincoln's behavior that I cannot muster respectful terms in which to write him."

Even so, Bryant was not so quick as other newspaper editors to abandon his early respect for the President. It was with great reluctance that he accepted his election to represent an indignant press to the President. In his book *Gotham Yankee* Harry Peckham describes the meeting in August 1862, at the White House:

> The President received the distinguished editor courteously, even cordially, and after a few pleasantries and a bad pun or two, assumed a properly serious air.
>
> . . . .
>
> . . . Bryant noticed that the man had aged considerably since that memorable February evening at Cooper Institute. Looking much older than his fifty-three years, Mr. Lincoln now wore a graying square chin beard. His mouth and forehead had gathered many wrinkles, and his tired eyes were a little bloodshot.
>
> . . . .
>
> The President listened patiently, even appreciatively, to what Bryant had to say. . . . But Lincoln was exasperatingly vague and indecisive about methods. . . . a few weeks later, Bryant was again inveighing editorially against "the weakness and vacillation of the Administration."

And on August 19 Horace Greeley published over his signature in the *Tribune* the now famous open letter to the President, "The Prayer of Twenty Millions," in which he vigorously insisted that Lincoln once for all commit himself definitely to emancipation.

One month later Lincoln responded to the need the

newspaper men, Lowell, Greeley, and Bryant, regarded as most urgent. On September 22 Lincoln announced the Emancipation Proclamation, and though it was not to be official until the first day of the new year Bryant's confidence in the President promptly returned. The humanitarian poet and liberal newspaper editor now regarded him as "perhaps the noblest statesman that the country had ever known." Bryant, a supporter of John Brown, had always favored immediate emancipation. And now he wrote a poem celebrating the event, "The Death of Slavery."

It was this last feeling for the man which inspired the tender tribute "The Death of Lincoln." The little lyric, genuine and spontaneous, expressed the feeling of the nation. It was penned immediately after the assassination and read, together with Lincoln's Second Inaugural Address, at the Union Square services following the funeral procession in New York City. It first appeared in print the next January when it was accepted for *The Atlantic Monthly*.

THE DEATH OF LINCOLN

Oh, slow to smite and swift to spare,
*   Gentle and merciful and just!*
Who, in the fear of God, didst bear
*   The sword of power, a nation's trust!*

In sorrow by thy bier we stand,
*   Amid the awe that hushes all,*
And speak the anguish of a land
*   That shook with horror at thy fall.*

Thy task is done; the bond are free:
*   We bear thee to an honored grave,*

Whose proudest monument shall be
  The broken fetters of the slave.

Pure was thy life; its bloody close
  Hath placed thee with the sons of light,
Among the noble host of those
  Who perished in the cause of Right.

Richard Henry Stoddard

1825–1903

D URING the Civil War Richard Henry Stoddard served as literary editor of the New York *World*. As such he made and perpetuated close friendships with most of the important men of letters in the country, among them his fellow poets Edmund Clarence Stedman and William Cullen Bryant. When Stoddard completed his "Abraham Lincoln: An Horatian Ode," Stedman, who had himself written an elegy for Lincoln, remarked on it in terms of the highest praise. He was not comparing it only to other poems on the subject of Lincoln when he declared: "I think his magnificent Monody or Horatian Ode unequalled by any previous American poem, and if it is not so deemed by the press and public, it will be a cruel renewal of the injustice which has been the lot of all young New York poets." And at the turn of the century when he edited his *American Anthology* Stedman was careful to include this poem.

Stoddard produced a second panegyric for the dead President, a kind of lyrical character sketch beginning, "This man whose homely face you look upon. . . ." But the Ode is clearly the superior tribute. The distinctive thing about the poem is that it does not insist on Lincoln's perfection. It makes no attempt to associate him with Christ; the poet does not wink at his faults, nor apologize for them. The result is that Lincoln is made all the more impressive as man and as President. For Stoddard "Perhaps he was not great— / But he preserved the State!" He was

6

the President, who "Often appeared to halt, / And was, of course, at fault: / Heard all opinions, nothing loath, / And loving both sides, angered both." With rustic manners and uncouth speech, with thoughts which were the thoughts of other men, he was "most unfit," no hero of the Roman mould. And this was the man who had saved the Union, to whose tomb "his countrymen shall come, / With memory proud, with pity dumb, / And strangers far and near, / For many and many a year!"

Perhaps Stoddard never wrote a finer poem; certainly it is one of his very few really accomplished compositions. And although it is not one of America's most imperishable poems it retains a certain charm even to this day. The tone is right, and the sentiment is right; and the lyrical effect of the stanza shape, with the two tetrameter lines followed by the two shorter trimeter lines, is considerable. The opening is impressive and the quiet close is serenely beautiful.

ABRAHAM LINCOLN: AN HORATIAN ODE

Not as when some great Captain falls
In battle, where his Country calls,
    Beyond the struggling lines
    That push his dread designs

To doom, by some stray ball struck dead:
Or, in the last charge, at the head
    Of his determined men,
    Who must be victors then.

Nor as when sink the civic great,
The safer pillars of the State,
    Whose calm, mature, wise words
    Suppress the need of swords.

With no such tears as e'er were shed
Above the noblest of our dead
    Do we to-day deplore
    The Man that is no more.

Our sorrow hath a wider scope,
Too strange for fear, too vast for hope,
    A wonder, blind and dumb,
    That waits—what is to come!

Not more astounded had we been
If Madness, that dark night, unseen,
    Had in our chambers crept,
    And murdered while we slept!

We woke to find a mourning earth,
Our Lares shivered on the hearth,
    The roof-tree fallen, all
    That could affright, appall!

Such thunderbolts, in other lands,
Have smitten the rod from royal hands,
    But spared, with us, till now,
    Each laurelled Caesar's brow.

No Caesar he whom we lament,
A Man without a precedent,
    Sent, it would seem, to do
    His work, and perish, too.

Not by the weary cares of State,
The endless tasks, which will not wait,
    Which, often done in vain,
    Must yet be done again:

Not in the dark, wild tide of war,
Which rose so high, and rolled so far,
    Sweeping from sea to sea
    In awful anarchy:

Four fateful years of mortal strife,
Which slowly drained the nation's life,
  (Yet for each drop that ran
  There sprang an armëd man!)

Not then; but when, by measures meet,
By victory, and by defeat,
  By courage, patience, skill,
  The people's fixed "We will!"

Had pierced, had crushed Rebellion dead,
Without a hand, without a head,
  At last, when all was well,
  He fell, O how he fell!

The time, the place, the stealing shape,
The coward shot, the swift escape,
  The wife—the widow's scream,—
  It is a hideous Dream!

A dream? What means this pageant, then?
These multitudes of solemn men,
  Who speak not when they meet,
  But throng the silent street?

The flags half-mast that late so high
Flaunted at each new victory?
  (The stars no brightness shed,
  But bloody looks the red!)

The black festoons that stretch for miles,
And turn the streets to funeral aisles?
  (No house too poor to show
  The nation's badge of woe.)

The cannon's sudden, sullen boom,
The bells that toll of death and doom,
  The rolling of the drums,
  The dreadful car that comes?

Cursed be the hand that fired the shot,
The frenzied brain that hatched the plot,
　Thy country's Father slain
　By thee, thou worse than Cain!

Tyrants have fallen by such as thou,
And good hath followed—may it now!
　(God lets bad instruments
　Produce the best events.)

But he, the man we mourn to-day,
No tyrant was: so mild a sway
　In one such weight who bore
　Was never known before.

Cool should he be, of balanced powers,
The ruler of a race like ours,
　Impatient, headstrong, wild,
　The Man to guide the Child.

And this he was, who most unfit
(So hard the sense of God to hit,)
　Did seem to fill his place;
　With such a homely face,

Such rustic manners, speech uncouth,
(That somehow blundered out the truth,)
　Untried, untrained to bear
　The more than kingly care.

Ah! And his genius put to scorn
The proudest in the purple born,
　Whose wisdom never grew
　To what, untaught, he knew,

The People, of whom he was one:
No gentleman, like Washington,
　(Whose bones, methinks, make room,
　To have him in their tomb!)

A laboring man, with horny hands,
Who swung the axe, who tilled his lands,
   Who shrank from nothing new,
   But did as poor men do.

One of the People! Born to be
Their curious epitome;
   To share yet rise above
   Their shifting hate and love.

Common his mind, (it seemed so then,)
His thoughts the thoughts of other men:
   Plain were his words, and poor,
   But now they will endure!

No hasty fool, of stubborn will,
But prudent, cautious, pliant still;
   Who since his work was good
   Would do it as he could.

Doubting, was not ashamed to doubt,
And, lacking prescience, went without:
   Often appeared to halt,
   And was, of course, at fault;

Heard all opinions, nothing loath,
And, loving both sides, angered both:
   Was—not like Justice, blind,
   But watchful, clement, kind.

No hero this of Roman mould,
Nor like our stately sires of old:
   Perhaps he was not great,
   But he preserved the State!

O honest face, which all men knew!
O tender heart, but known to few!
   O wonder of the age,
   Cut off by tragic rage!

Peace! Let the long procession come,
For hark, the mournful, muffled drum,
   The trumpet's wail afar,
   And see, the awful car!

Peace! Let the sad procession go,
While cannon boom and bells toll slow.
   And go, thou sacred car,
   Bearing our woe afar!

Go, darkly borne, from State to State,
Whose loyal, sorrowing cities wait
   To honor all they can
   The dust of that good man.

Go, grandly borne, with such a train
As greatest kings might die to gain.
   The just, the wise, the brave,
   Attend thee to the grave.

And you, the soldiers of our wars,
Bronzed veterans, grim with noble scars,
   Salute him once again,
   Your late commander—slain!

Yes, let your tears indignant fall,
But leave your muskets on the wall;
   Your country needs you now
   Beside the forge—the plough.

(When Justice shall unsheathe her brand,—
If Mercy may not stay her hand,
   Nor would we have it so,—
   She must direct the blow.)

And you, amid the master-race,
Who seem so strangely out of place,
   Know ye who cometh? He
   Who hath declared ye free.

Bow while the body passes—nay,
Fall on your knees, and weep, and pray!
  Weep, weep—I would ye might—
  Your poor black faces white!

And, children, you must come in bands,
With garlands in your little hands,
  Of blue and white and red,
  To strew before the dead.

So sweetly, sadly, sternly goes
The Fallen to his last repose.
  Beneath no mighty dome,
  But in his modest home;

The churchyard where his children rest,
The quiet spot that suits him best,
  There shall his grave be made,
  And there his bones be laid.

And there his countrymen shall come,
With memory proud, with pity dumb,
  And strangers far and near,
  For many and many a year.

For many a year and many an age,
While History on her ample page
  The virtues shall enroll
  Of that Paternal Soul.

Edmund Clarence Stedman

1833–1908

Edmund Clarence Stedman, poet, critic, journalist, broker, was very close to the Civil War and very close, too, to both of the principals in the April 14th tragedy, Abraham Lincoln and John Wilkes Booth.

Stedman, who had written a poem "How Old John Brown Took Harper's Ferry," was, like Bryant, sympathetic with the Abolitionist cause. He felt the war to be a duty on the part of the North, and was the first war correspondent to reach the capital at Washington. Thereafter he served with the Army of the Potomac as a reporter from the Headquarters of Generals McDowell and McClellan.

He had lamented the outbreak of hostilities with a poem, "The Twelfth of April," afterwards entitled simply "Sumter," which he wrote on the morning of Saturday, April 13. The lyric was published that same day in the evening issue of the *World*, the newly begun paper which he had been serving, and again on the following Wednesday in the morning edition. Thus it was the first poem to come out of the war.[6]

Earlier, on June 13, 1860, he had published in the *Press and Tribune* of Chicago and in the *Weekly Illinois State Journal* a lyric entitled "Honest Abe of the West." It proved to be immensely popular and was sung throughout the campaign to the tune of "The Star Spangled Banner."

[6] See Laura Stedman and George M. Gould, *Life and Letters of Edmund Clarence Stedman* (New York: Moffatt, Yard and Co., 1910), I, 223.

On September 6, 1862, when the war was going badly for the North, Stedman appealed to the President in a poem called "Wanted—A Man." The poem, printed in Horace Greeley's *Tribune* three days later, was delivered at that time into the hands of President Lincoln, who read it to his Cabinet. Stedman's biographers tell us that the stanzas, "voicing the urgent need of the North for a great leader," were repeated throughout the country.

WANTED—A MAN

Back from the trebly crimsoned field
   Terrible words are thunder-tost;
Full of the wrath that will not yield,
   Full of revenge for battles lost!
   Hark to their echo, as it crost
The Capital, making faces wan:
   "End this murderous holocaust;
Abraham Lincoln, give us a MAN!

"Give us a man of God's own mould,
   Born to marshal his fellow-men;
One whose fame is not bought and sold
   At the stroke of a politician's pen;
   Give us the man of thousands ten,
Fit to do as well as to plan;
   Give us a rallying-cry, and then,
Abraham Lincoln, give us a MAN!

"No leader to shirk the boasting foe,
   And to march and countermarch our brave,
Till they fall like ghosts in the marshes low,
   And swamp-grass covers each nameless grave;
   Nor another, whose fatal banners wave
Aye in Disaster's shameful van;

Nor another, to bluster, and lie, and rave;—
Abraham Lincoln, give us a MAN!

"Hearts are mourning in the North,
   While the sister rivers seek the main,
Red with our life-blood flowing forth,—
   Who shall gather it up again?
   Though we march to the battle-plain
Firmly as when the strife began,
   Shall all our offering be in vain?—
Abraham Lincoln, give us a MAN!

"Is there never one in all the land,
   One on whose might the Course may lean?
Are all the common ones so grand,
   And all the titled ones so mean?
   What if your failure may have been
In trying to make good bread from bran,
   From worthless metal a weapon keen?—
Abraham Lincoln, find us a MAN!

"O, we will follow him to the death,
   Where the foeman's fiercest columns are!
O, we will use our latest breath,
   Cheering for every sacred star!
   His to marshal us high and far;
Ours to battle, as patriots can
   When a Hero leads the Holy War!—
Abraham Lincoln, give us a MAN!"

One week after the assassination, Stedman, in a letter to his good friend Bayard Taylor, describes the mood of the city:

I would that you were here to see this town, converted into a vast mausoleum by the national calamity. You know that a *vulgar* woman appears a lady *in mourning;* and that a lady is never so elegant as when in black. Something of the same effect has been produced on our superb, but bizarre and inharmonious, city. It looks like an immense black and white flower, with leaves and petals spreading grandly and in perfect keeping, to every point of the compass. Such an effect I never saw, or dreamed of. It is overwhelming, sombre, sublime. Just the same feeling, of the spirit of which all this is the outward symbol, flows like a mighty river through the hearts of the million. It can never be changed or lessened. The South has sinned the "unpardonable sin."—To me the history of the last four years seems as fateful and tragic as all the Greek Dramas rolled into one, and applied to nations instead of families. The "unities" of the terrible play have been faultlessly preserved. It is as perfect in climax, as it is gigantic, and its effects on the future of human progress are palpable to all of us whose eyes were ever anointed to discern the right and the sure.[7]

Stedman had already, in this same spirit, produced a sonnet on the assassination. In response to a request of a friend of his, thirty-three years later, actually on the birthdate of Abraham Lincoln, the poet copied down the lines and attached some interesting comments on Edwin Booth, the celebrated Shakespearean actor and elder brother to the assassin:

By a strange coincidence—most certainly without provision on my part—I have copied the Lincoln Sonnet for you at this Club [The Players] founded by the gentle, patriotic, eminent man of genius, Edwin Booth,—and from the volume of my early poems which he owned, and had preserved in his library; moreover, I have fulfilled your wish, it seems, upon the anniversary of the birth of the man whose martyrdom the sonnet denounced.

Having observed all this, I am somewhat awed and self-reproachful, as if I were disloyal to the manes of my dear friend. I never shall copy the sonnet again, and probably shall not retain it in future collections of my verse [?].

I hesitate as to sending it, though promised, even to you. Yet perhaps this is the occasion for putting on record that its outcry for the revenge which Bacon calls "a kind of wild Justice" was under the prevailing misconception that Southern policy

[7] Stedman and Gould, I, 352–353.

brought about the assassination; also, that Edwin Booth (with whom I was of equal age), over whose after-life that tragedy imposed such a cloud of melancholy, comprehended all, and of his own volition, a year later, became my attached comrade— and loyal comrades we remained until his dying day.[8]

The sonnet had been published in the *Tribune* the morning before the day of the funeral. Its first line identifies Lincoln's martyrdom with that of Christ, and echoes of Lincoln's Second Inaugural Address ring through the lyric.

ABRAHAM LINCOLN

Assassinated Good Friday, 1865

"Forgive them, for they know not what they do!"
He said, and so went shriven to his fate,—
Unknowing went, that generous heart and true.
Even while he spoke the slayer lay in wait,
And when the morning opened Heaven's gate
There passed the whitest soul a nation knew.
Henceforth all thoughts of pardon are too late;
They, in whose cause that arm its weapon drew,
Have murdered Mercy. Now alone shall stand
Blind Justice, with the sword unsheathed she wore.
Hark, from the eastern to the western strand,
The swelling thunder of the people's roar:
What words they murmur,—Fetter not her hand!
So let it smite, such deeds shall be no more!

Years later Stedman produced still another memorial to Lincoln. Called "The Hand of Lincoln," the poem makes Lincoln's hand into a mighty symbol of strength, and tenderness, and liberty.

[8] Stedman and Gould, I, 353–354.

THE HAND OF LINCOLN

Look on this cast, and know the hand
   That bore a nation in its hold:
From this mute witness understand
   What Lincoln was,—how large of mould

The man who sped the woodman's team,
   And deepest sunk the ploughman's share,
And pushed the laden raft astream,
   Of fate before him unaware.

This was the hand that knew to swing
   The axe—since thus would Freedom train
Her son—and made the forest ring,
   And drove the wedge, and toiled amain.

Firm hand, that loftier office took,
   A conscious leader's will obeyed,
And, when men sought his word and look,
   With steadfast might the gathering swayed.

No courtier's, toying with a sword,
   Nor minstrel's, laid across a lute;
A chief's, uplifted to the Lord
   When all the kings of earth were mute!

The hand of Anak, sinewed strong,
   The fingers that on greatness clutch;
Yet, lo! the marks their lines along
   Of one who strove and suffered much.

For here in knotted cord and vein
   I trace the varying chart of years;
I know the troubled heart, the strain,
   The weight of Atlas—and the tears.

Again I see the patient brow
   That palm erewhile was wont to press;

And now 't is furrowed deep, and now
   Made smooth with hope and tenderness.

For something of a formless grace
   This moulded outline plays about;
A pitying flame, beyond our trace,
   Breathes like a spirit, in and out,—

The love that cast an aureole
   Round one who, longer to endure,
Called mirth to ease his ceaseless dole,
   Yet kept his nobler purpose sure.

Lo, as I gaze, the statured man,
   Built up from yon large hand, appears:
A type that Nature wills to plan
   But once in all a people's years.

What better than this voiceless cast
   To tell of such a one as he,
Since through its living semblance passed
   The thought that bade a race be free!

John Greenleaf Whittier
1807–1892

J OHN GREENLEAF WHITTIER, the energetic New England
Quaker-Abolitionist, is perhaps best thought of as a
newspaper poet. More than any other writer of the time
Whittier turned out verse in the interest of political and
social reform. Most of his poetry was produced in haste,
to comment on the occasion; little was revised. Besides,
Whittier's ear was notoriously poor. Thus we have from his
pen no really memorable contribution to the Lincoln poetry. Nevertheless, at least one of his poems yet deserves
close attention as a tribute to Lincoln, and Whittier's role
in the war and his attitude toward the President are interesting.

Naturally the pacifist Whittier resisted the coming of the
war. But when it appeared to him inevitable he threw his
influence behind Lincoln, and when it actually arrived he
described in detail the work required of the pacifist Quak-
ers, a role not unlike that assumed by Walt Whitman,
himself half a Quaker: "We have no right to ask or to
expect an exemption . . . we owe it to the cause of truth,
to show that exalted heroism and generous self-sacrifice are
not incompatible with our pacific principles. Our mission is,
at this time, to mitigate the sufferings of our countrymen,
to visit and aid the sick and the wounded, to relieve the
necessities of the widow and the orphan, and to practice
economy for the sake of charity."

Of course for Whittier himself a more active part was

natural. For him the first thing was the emancipation of the slaves, and to this end he had worked tirelessly from the beginning of the trouble. He had already written a host of intensely acrid anti-slavery poems, such as "From Massachusetts to Virginia," and he was so incensed by the Fugitive Slave Law, which Webster had permitted in the Compromise of 1850, that in one of his most powerful poems he labeled a traitor the great Senator whom he had loved.

When General Frémont, whom Whittier had supported for the Republican nomination of 1856, issued during the war a military order emancipating all slaves in his department, the President promptly censured him, countermanding the order himself when Frémont refused to do so. Whittier just as promptly came to Frémont's defense and he continued thereafter to agitate for immediate emancipation.

One of the hymns Whittier wrote at the very beginning of the war, usually called "The Furnace Blast," was so strong in its anti-slavery sentiment that it excited quite a commotion among Union soldiers and officers when it was sung among them after the first Battle of Bull Run. When Generals Kearney and McClellan ordered the hymn banned from Union Army camps, Mr. Hutchinson, leader of the group of singers, carried the matter through Secretary Chase to Lincoln himself. Whitman Bennett, one of Whittier's biographers, tells us that when Lincoln was informed of the difficulty and shown the poem in a Cabinet meeting, he declared at once that these were "just the songs he wanted his soldiers to hear."

But most of Whittier's war poems are of little value as poetry. They seem to be the products of weariness and discouragement, of a depressed state of mind. Certainly, whatever the reasons, they are not so good as the *Battle Pieces* of Melville or the *Drum Taps* of Walt Whitman.

Yet the pronouncement of the Emancipation produced

in him the same excitement Bryant experienced. He enjoyed an altogether new emotion, ecstasy almost: "We are living in a grand time; one year now is worth a dozen of the years of our ancestors." For Whittier, as for so many others, Lincoln was first of all the Great Emancipator. He was late to acknowledge, or even to recognize, the greatness of the President, but it is reported that, long years after the war, when he was shown the famous Marshall engraving of Lincoln, he observed, "It is the face of the speaker at Gettysburg and the writer of the second inaugural."

It was this feeling that inspired his lyric "The Proclamation," but his finest tribute to Lincoln appears in the poem entitled "The Emancipation Group." Moses Kimball, a citizen of Boston, had presented to that city a duplicate of the Freedman's Memorial Statue, which stands in the Lincoln Park in the nation's capital. Whittier wrote his poem on December 9, 1879, for the unveiling of the impressive statue. The lyric identifies Lincoln with Nature and the will of God. It is a paean to Freedom and a pledge to make good the sacrifice of the President.

THE EMANCIPATION GROUP

Amidst thy sacred effigies
Of old renown give place,
O city, Freedom-loved! to his
Whose hand unchained a race.

Take the worn frame, that rested not
Save in a martyr's grave—
The care-lined face, that none forgot,
Bent to the kneeling slave.

Let man be free! The mighty word
He spoke was not his own;

An impulse from the Highest stirred
   These chiselled lips alone.

The cloudy sign, the fiery guide,
   Along his pathway ran,
And Nature, through his voice, denied
   The ownership of man.

We rest in peace where these sad eyes
   Saw peril, strife, and pain;
His was the nation's sacrifice,
   And ours the priceless gain.

O symbol of God's will on earth
   As it is done above!
Bear witness to the cost and worth
   Of justice and of love.

Stand in thy place and testify
   To coming ages long,
That truth is stronger than a lie,
   And righteousness than wrong.

Oliver Wendell Holmes
1809–1894

EVERYBODY knows in what affection President Lincoln held the little lyric that Oliver Wendell Holmes had written on the figure of Major Thomas Melville, grandfather of Herman Melville. Lincoln knew "The Last Leaf" by heart and loved to recite it. He is supposed to have said on one occasion after he had repeated the poem that "For pure pathos, in my judgment, there is nothing finer than those six lines [the fourth stanza] in the English language."

In November of 1866 in a letter to John Morse, a Boston lawyer who was later to produce biographies of both Lincoln and Holmes, the poet revealed what Lincoln's interest in the lyric meant to him:

Governor Andrew once told me that the President recited *The Last Leaf* to him, entire, from memory. It will insure the memory of that poem, at least, and if everything else I have written shall be forgotten I think it will be long before a poem that such a man loved to repeat will be read with indifference. It would certainly be very grateful to me to have that poem of my youth embalmed by association with the memory of the best loved man of our generation; I might also say of our history.

Many years later, in July of 1891, to Henry C. Whitney, who had confirmed for Holmes through Lincoln's law-partner Herndon the intelligence that Lincoln was fond of the poem, the poet again discloses his great pleasure:

I cannot too warmly thank you for your kind letter enclosing that of your correspondent, the late Mr. Herndon. I have had many pleasant things said to me in the course of my long life, —very few so peculiarly gratifying as this containing the story of Mr. Lincoln's partiality for my poem, *The Last Leaf*. To have inspired such feelings in such a man is enough to palliate many literary shortcomings. I had heard from Governor Andrew that Mr. Lincoln was fond of the poem—that he knew it by heart and recited it to him. But I am very glad to have the fact again mentioned in the language of one who knew him well and would not be likely to exaggerate in telling the story.

The Professor of the Breakfast Table and the President were the same age, but apparently they never had any opportunity to meet. We do know that the poet's son did on one occasion meet Lincoln. As an officer in the Army of the Potomac he had been in Lincoln's presence for a short time at Fort Stevens, which the President had come to inspect. In fact, he is supposed to have spoken sharply to the Commander-in-chief when Lincoln somewhat foolishly exposed himself to enemy fire.

But Oliver Wendell Holmes was moved in a most personal way on news of the assassination. He had already written a very stirring "Hymn after the Emancipation Proclamation" when he was called upon to provide a eulogy for formal services held in Boston in memory of Abraham Lincoln. The memorial services were held on Thursday, June 1, 1865, at three o'clock in the afternoon at the Music Hall. Presiding over the services was the mayor of the city, whose name was also Lincoln, and delivering the address was the Honorable Charles Sumner. Holmes's ode was sung to the music of Luther's "Judgment Hymn." It is a plaintive prayer that the sacrifice of Lincoln shall not be in vain.

IN MEMORY OF ABRAHAM LINCOLN

(City of Boston, June 1, 1865)

O Thou of soul and sense and breath,
   The ever-present Giver,
Unto Thy mighty angel, death,
   All flesh Thou didst deliver;
What most we cherish, we resign,
For life and death alike are Thine,
   Who reignest Lord forever!

Our hearts lie buried in the dust
   With him, so true and tender,
The patriot's stay, the people's trust,
   The shield of the offender;
Yet every murmuring voice is still,
As, bowing to Thy sovereign will,
   Our best loved we surrender.

Dear Lord, with pitying eye behold
   This martyr generation,
Which Thou, through trials manifold,
   Art showing Thy salvation!
O let the blood by murder spilt
Wash out Thy stricken children's guilt,
   And sanctify our Nation!

Be Thou Thy orphaned Israel's friend,
   Forsake Thy people never,
In one our broken many blend,
   That none again may sever!
Hear us, O Father, while we raise
With trembling lips our song of praise,
   And bless Thy name forever!

James Russell Lowell

1819–1891

Yankee Lowell, an ardent Abolitionist, wrote often as editor of *The Atlantic Monthly* and *North American Review* in support of Lincoln's policies. He provided in his lecture on democracy a substantial impression of the character of the President, and in numerous articles and sketches he remarked on the capacities and qualities of Lincoln as man and as chief executive. Perhaps better than anyone else among his fellows Lowell felt intuitively the greatness of the President. But, like Bryant, he was led sometimes by what he heard and by what he saw into registering misgivings.

During the dark months of 1863 the poet's enthusiasm for the President began to wane. To a friend he confided privately: "Lincoln may be right for aught I know, but I guess an ounce of Frémont is worth a pound of Long Abraham. Mr. Lincoln seems to have the theory of carrying on the war without hurting the enemy. He is incapable, of understanding that they ought to be hurt."

But in January of 1864 in an article for the *North American Review* he sketched Lincoln as ". . . so gently guiding public sentiment that he seems to follow it, by so yielding doubtful points that he can be firm without seeming obstinate in essential ones." The article, later condensed for *My Study Windows* under the title "Abraham Lincoln," is full of praise for the President: Lowell speaks of "the good sense, the good humor, the sagacity, the large mindedness, and the unselfish honesty of the unknown man whom a blind fortune, as it seemed, has lifted from the crowd to the most dangerous and difficult eminence of modern times."

Happily, the President was able to enjoy the essay when it appeared in the *North American Review*. In a letter dated January 16, 1864, Lincoln, with his wonderful sense of humor and the good grace that regularly characterized him, called attention to the essay: "Of course I am not the most impartial judge, yet, with due allowance for this, I venture to hope that the article entitled 'The President's Policy' will be of value to the country. I fear I am not quite worthy of all which is therein said of me personally." [9]

Walt Whitman in *Song of Myself* employed the capital "I" in the sense of all humanity, but without success for his early readers. But Lowell declares that Lincoln could use the capital "I" without egoism or apology, the first such President. In his mouth, says Lowell, it seemed to mean "a collective multitude."

Carl Sandburg in *The War Years* cites Lowell's now-famous tribute to the President: "His kingship was conspicuous by its workday homespun. Never was ruler so absolute as he, nor so little conscious of it; for he was the incarnate common-sense of the people."

However, with the war dragging on and on in the wearisome sieges of Richmond and Petersburg, Lowell in the summer of 1864 revealed a precarious faith in the President: "The war and its constant expectations and anxieties oppress me. I cannot think. I hear bad things about Mr. Lincoln and try not to believe them." And then, at almost the same time, July 28, 1864, when an anxious nation looked to the coming election, he wrote to John Lothrop Motley, then in Europe, to apprise him of the situation in

[9] See Sandburg, *The War Years*, p. 452; also Harkness and McMurtry, pp. 93–95.

the states: "If Mr. Lincoln is re-chosen, I think the war will soon be over. . . . So far as I can see, the opposition to Mr. Lincoln is both selfish and factious."

Months after the close of the war and after the assassination of Lincoln, there was held at Harvard College, on July 21, 1865, a commemoration service for students and graduates of the College lost in the war. Two of these were nephews of James Russell Lowell, and he had lost also a third nephew. As Harvard's Professor-Poet he had been called on to write and to read a commemoration ode. He assented, but apparently had great difficulty in completing the poem, finishing it only the day before the memorial service.

Something of the poem's inception can be gleaned from a communication addressed to Richard Watson Gilder, who had himself written a lyric to the memory of Abraham Lincoln. In the letter, written more than twenty years after the event, Lowell referred to the ode as "an improvisation" and described its composition: "Two days before the Commemoration I had told my friend Child that it was impossible—that I was dull as a door-mat. But the next day something gave me a jog and the whole thing came with a rush. I sat up all night writing it out clear. . . ." He noted especially the prodigious speed with which he wrote, remarking that his pencil rarely hesitated or made a correction afterwards.

The commemoration services were held in the open air. Prominent among the speakers were Major-General Meade, the hero of Gettysburg, and Major-General Devens. The summer afternoon was drawing to a close when the poet began to recite his ode. Observers later remarked that Lowell's face was glowing, that he was almost transfigured. Reports testify that the effect was overpowering.

One of Lowell's biographers, Ferris Greenslet, has remarked that a great occasion "sublimed Lowell into a great poet." In the "Commemoration Ode," declares Greenslet, Lowell's poetry "wins to a 'high immunity from night.' Until the dream of human brotherhood is forgotten, the echo of its large music will not wholly die away."

Probably the most impressive passage of this beautiful Ode, which was dedicated in its first printing "to the ever sweet and shining memory of the ninety-three sons of Harvard College who have died for their country in the war of nationality," are the last few lines of Section V and all of Section VI, an elegy for the nation's Martyr-Chief, just three months dead.

from
ODE RECITED AT THE HARVARD COMMEMORATION

Life may be given in many ways,
    And loyalty to Truth be sealed
As bravely in the closet as the field,
      So bountiful is Fate;
      But then to stand beside her,
      When craven churls deride her,
To front a lie in arms and not to yield,
      This shows, methinks, God's plan
      And measure of a stalwart man,
      Limbed like the old heroic breeds,
      Who stands self-poised on manhood's solid earth,
    Not forced to frame excuses for his birth,
Fed from within with all the strength he needs.

Such was he, our Martyr-Chief,
      Whom late the Nation he had led,
      With ashes on her head,
Wept with the passion of an angry grief:

Forgive me, if from present things I turn
To speak what in my heart will beat and burn,
And hang my wreath on his world-honored urn.
    Nature, they say, doth dote,
    And cannot make a man
    Save on some worn-out plan,
    Repeating us by rote:
For him her Old-World moulds aside she threw,
    And, choosing sweet clay from the breast
    Of the unexhausted West,
With stuff untainted shaped a hero new,
Wise, steadfast in the strength of God, and true.
    How beautiful to see
Once more a shepherd of mankind indeed,
Who loved his charge, but never loved to lead;
One whose meek flock the people joyed to be,
    Not lured by any cheat of birth,
    But by his clear-grained human worth,
And brave old wisdom of sincerity!
    They knew that outward grace is dust;
    They could not choose but trust
In that sure-footed mind's unfaltering skill,
    And supple-tempered will
That bent like perfect steel to spring again and thrust.
    His was no lonely mountain-peak of mind,
    Thrusting to thin air o'er our cloudy bars,
    A sea-mark now, now lost in vapors blind;
    Broad prairie rather, genial, level-lined,
    Fruitful and friendly for all human kind,
Yet also nigh to heaven and loved of loftiest stars.
    Nothing of Europe here,
Or, then, of Europe fronting mornward still,
    Ere any names of Serf and Peer
    Could Nature's equal scheme deface
    And thwart her genial will;

Here was a type of the true elder race,
And one of Plutarch's men talked with us face to face.
   I praise him not; it were too late;
And some innative weakness there must be
In him who condescends to victory
Such as the Present gives, and cannot wait,
   Safe in himself as in a fate.
     So always firmly he:
     He knew to bide his time,
     And can his fame abide,
Still patient in his simple faith sublime,
     Till the wise years decide.
   Great captains, with their guns and drums,
   Disturb our judgment for the hour,
     But at last silence comes;
These all are gone, and, standing like a tower,
Our children shall behold his fame.
   The kindly-earnest, brave, foreseeing man,
Sagacious, patient, dreading praise, not blame,
   New birth of our new soil, the first American.

Walt Whitman

1819–1892

I T was most fitting that Walt Whitman should compose *the* elegy for Abraham Lincoln. First, Walt Whitman among all the poets of America most plainly expresses the spirit of democracy, as Abraham Lincoln among all political figures has come most plainly to embody the ideal of democracy. Second, Whitman passionately admired the President and had not to wait the assassination, as others did, to appreciate his greatness. Third, through the war years the poet as wound-dresser in the hospitals around Washington was in a position to study the President's conduct of the war and the effect of the war upon the President. Finally, in April of 1865 Walt Whitman's was the most genuine and most lyrical poetic voice in America.

To this day the details of the actual Lincoln-Whitman relationship are immersed in confusion. Three aspects of the relationship are most talked about. One popular idea is that Lincoln in his Springfield law office did one day read aloud from *Leaves of Grass* to some law students and to William H. Herndon, his friend and law partner (later the subject of a poem by Edgar Lee Masters). Another notion, made popular by W. D. O'Connor, enthusiastic author of *The Good Gray Poet*, is that Lincoln did on one occasion, having seen the poet pass by, remark to a companion, "Well, *he* looks like a MAN!" And then there are Whitman's own remarks made in his late years which suggest that he was more than a nodding acquaintance with the

President. He writes, for example, in *November Boughs*, that "it was my fortune through 1862 to '65 to see, or pass a word with, or watch him, personally, perhaps twenty or thirty times."

Much doubt has been cast on all these things, and it would seem that Whitman and Lincoln did not actually know each other personally, that probably there was never a word exchanged between them. Nevertheless, there existed a spiritual kinship that no one would dispute. And the poet had every right to insist, as he did, that "Lincoln belongs to me."

Whitman's most vivid impressions of Lincoln are set down in a series of letters addressed to his mother during the time he was serving as a wound-dresser in the Washington hospitals. One such communication, dated June 30, 1863, includes a hint that the poet feared for the life of the President:

Mr. Lincoln passes here (14th St.) every evening on his way out [to the Soldiers' Home]. I noticed him last evening about half-past 6—he was in his barouche, two horses, guarded by about thirty cavalry. The barouche comes first under a slow trot, driven by one man in the box, no servant or footman beside; the cavalry all follow closely after with a lieutenant at their head. I had a good view of the President last evening. He looks more careworn even than usual, his face with deep cut lines, seams, and his *complexion gray* through very dark skin—a curious looking man, very sad. I said to a lady who was looking with me, "Who can see that man without losing all wish to be sharp upon him personally?". . . . The President dresses in plain black clothes, cylinder hat—he was alone yesterday. As he came up he first drove over to the house of the Sec. of War, on K St., about 300 feet from here; sat in his carriage while Stanton came out and had a 15 minutes interview with him (I can see from my window), and then wheeled around the corner and up Fourteenth St., the cavalry after him. I really think it would be safer for him just now to stop at the White House, but I expect he is too proud to abandon the former custom.

In the fall of the same year, after the Battle of Gettysburg, again the poet remarks on Lincoln to his mother:

I have finally made up my mind that Mr. Lincoln has done as good as a human man could do. I still think him a pretty big President. I realize here in Washington that it has been a big thing to have just kept the United States from being thrown down and having its throat cut; and now I have no doubt it will throw down Secession and cut its throat—and I have not had any doubt since Gettysburg.

For *Specimen Days*, an autobiographical work appearing in 1882, Whitman brought together a collection of entries from notebooks, journals, and diaries, and some passages from earlier personal essays. In the war memoranda, which, the poet says, are "verbatim copies of those lurid and blood-smutch'd little note-books" that he had kept faithfully during his experiences in the war hospitals, occur vivid recollections of the President and the war wounded. One passage, dated February 24, 1863, is a paean to the White House:

A spell of fine soft weather. I wander about a good deal, some- times at night under the moon. To-night took a long look at the President's house. The white portico—the palace-like, tall, round columns, spotless as snow—the walls also—the tender and soft moonlight, flooding the pale marble, and making peculiar faint languishing shades, not shadows—everywhere a soft trans- parent hazy, thin blue moon-lace, hanging in the air—the brilliant and extra-plentiful clusters of gas, on and around the façade, columns, portico, &c.—everything so white, so marbly pure and dazzling, yet soft—the White House of future poems, and of dreams and dramas, there in the soft and copious moon —the gorgeous front, in the trees, under the lustrous flooding moon, full of reality, full of illusion—the forms of the trees, leafless, silent, in trunk and myriad-angles of branches, under the stars and sky—the White House of the land, and of beauty and night—sentries at the gates, and, by the portico, silent, pacing there in blue overcoats—stopping you not at all, but eyeing you with sharp eyes, whichever way you move.

Later that year, on August 12, Whitman addressed to the New York *Times* a kind of composite impression of Lincoln which closes with the poet's impression of the President as seen in a passing carriage:

. . . I saw the President in the face fully . . . and his look, though abstracted, happen'd to be directed steadily in my eye. He bow'd and smiled, but far beneath his smile I noticed well the expression I have alluded to. None of the artists or pictures has caught the deep, though subtle and indirect expression of this man's face. There is something else there. One of the great portrait painters of two or three centuries ago is needed.

Some months later the poet wrote to a friend: "I believe fully in Lincoln—few know the rocks and quicksands he has to steer through."

In January 1865 he recorded his impressions of the inaugural levee at the White House, at which he was present, though he seems not to have shaken hands with the President as Herman Melville had done on the occasion of the first inaugural:

Never before was such a compact jam in front of the White House—all the grounds fill'd, and away out to the spacious sidewalks. I was there, as I took a notion to go—was in the rush inside with the crowd—surged along the passage-ways, the blue and other rooms, and through the great east-room. Crowds of country people, some very funny. Fine music from the Marine Band, off in a side place. I saw Mr. Lincoln, drest all in black, with white kid gloves and a claw-hammer coat, receiving, as in duty bound, shaking hands, looking very disconsolate, and as if he would give anything to be somewhere else.

Whitman anticipates his later metaphor of Lincoln as captain of the ship of state in a letter which Carl Sandburg tells us was sent off to two boys in New York in March:

I think well of the President. He has a face like a Hoosier Michael Angelo, so awful ugly it becomes beautiful, with its strange mouth, its deep cut, criss-cross lines, and its doughnut complexion. . . . I do not dwell on the supposed failures of his government; he has shown I sometimes think an almost supernatural tact in keeping the ship afloat at all.

For the day after the death of Abraham Lincoln the poet finds in his notes this passage on his going:

He leaves for America's history and biography, so far, not only its most dramatic reminiscence—he leaves, in my opinion, the greatest, best, most characteristic, artistic, moral personality. Not but that he had faults, and show'd them in the Presidency; but honesty, goodness, shrewdness, conscience, and (a new virtue, unknown to other lands, and hardly yet really known here, but the foundation and tie of all, as the future will grandly develop,) UNIONISM, in its truest and amplest sense, form'd the hard-pan of his character. These he seal'd with his life. The tragic splendor of his death, purging, illuminating all, throws round his form, his head, an aureole that will remain and will grow brighter through time, while history lives, and love of country lasts. By many has this Union been help'd; but if one name, one man, must be pick'd out, he, most of all, is the conservator of it, to the future. He was assassinated—but the Union is not assassinated—*ça ira!* One falls, and another falls. The soldier drops, sinks like a wave—but the ranks of the ocean eternally press on. Death does its work, obliterates a hundred, a thousand —President, general, captain, private—but the Nation is immortal.

Some six weeks later, while Whitman was still dutifully tending the convalescent of the war, he offers in his notes the account of an incident touching upon the feeling of the soldiers for their chief, the feeling that the poet tried to capture for his lyric "Hush'd Be the Camps To-day":

As I sat by the bedside of a sick Michigan soldier in hospital to-day, a convalescent from the adjoining bed rose and came to me, and presently we began talking. He was a middle-aged man, belonged to the 2d Virginia regiment, but lived in Racine, Ohio, and had a family there. He spoke of President Lincoln, and said: "The war is over, and many are lost. And now we have lost the best, the fairest, the truest man in America. Take him altogether, he was the best man this country ever produced.

It was quite a while I thought very different; but some time before the murder, that's the way I have seen it." There was deep earnestness in the soldier. (I found upon further talk he had known Mr. Lincoln personally, and quite closely, years before.) He was a veteran; was now in the fifth year of his service; was a cavalry man, and had been in a good deal of hard fighting.

But Whitman's most penetrating and most exhaustive analysis of Lincoln is to be found in a lecture which he prepared for the anniversary of the tragedy, a lecture he was to give nine times, in New York, Philadelphia, Boston, and Camden. The first lecture was delivered in New York, April 14, 1879, the last in Camden on April 14, 1890. The address includes the expression of his hope and desire, "till my own dying day, whenever the 14th or 15th of April comes, to annually gather a few friends, and hold its tragic reminiscence." He had earlier vowed he would every day of his life have sprigs of lilac for his room. He tells also of his first view of Abraham Lincoln and then reports on the changes apparent in the President during the four years following that date. In great detail, so vivid one would swear the poet had been in the theater that night (though he was not, and had the story from a streetcar conductor friend, Peter Doyle, who had seen it all from a balcony of the theater), he describes the fateful day of April 14. The lecture closes with Lowell's label for Lincoln, Martyr-Chief, and an accurate prophecy of the significance of his martyrdom when "leading historians and dramatists seek for some personage, some special event, incisive enough to mark with deepest cut, and mnemonize, this turbulent nineteenth century of ours, (not only these States, but all over the political and social world). . . ." Whitman insisted that historians would "seek in vain for any point to serve more thoroughly their purpose. . . ."

Edmund Clarence Stedman was in the New York audi-

ence which heard the first lecture. His description of the
poet and his address is affectionate and appreciative:

I was one of a small but sympathetic audience gathered in
New York to hear Mr. Whitman, at the cordial request of
authors, journalists, and artists, deliver a lecture upon
Abraham Lincoln. As he entered, haltingly, and took the seat
placed for him, his appearance satisfied the eye. His manly figure, clothed in a drab suit that loosely and well became him,
his head crowned with flowing silvery hair, his bearded, ruddy
and wholesome face, upon which sat a look of friendliness, the
wise benignity that comes with ripened years, all these gave
him the aspect of a poet and sage. His reminiscences of the
martyr President were slight, but he had read the hero's heart,
had sung his dirge, and no theme could have been dearer to him
or more fitly chosen. The lecture was written in panoramic,
somewhat disjoined prose, but its brokenness was the counter-
part of his vocal manner, with its frequent pauses, interphrases,
illustrations. His delivery was persuasive, natural, by turns
tender and strong, and he held us with him from the outset.
Something of Lincoln himself seemed to pass into this man who
had loved and studied him. A patriot of the honest school spoke
to us, yet with a new voice—a man who took the future into
his patriotism, and the world no less than his own land.

I wished that the youths of America could hear him, and that
he might go through the land, reading as he did that night,
from town to town. . . . When the brief discourse was ended,
he was induced to read the shorter dirge, "O Captain! My
Captain!" It is, of his poems, among those nearest to a wonted
lyrical form, as if the genuine sorrow of his theme had given
him new pinions. He read it simply and well, and as I listened
to its strange, pathetic melodies, my eyes filled with tears, and
I felt that here, indeed, was a minstrel of whom it would be
said, if he could reach the ears of the multitude and stand in
their presence, that not only the cultured, but "the common
people heard him gladly."

Whitman had first heard the news of the assassination in
the company of his mother at their Long Island home. The
great shock with which it was received he has himself
described: "The day of the murder we heard the news very

early in the morning. Mother prepared breakfast—and other meals afterwards—as usual; but not a mouthful was eaten all day by either of us. We each drank half a cup of coffee; that was all. Little was said. We got every newspaper morning and evening, and the frequent extras of that period, and pass'd them silently to each other."

In the time immediately subsequent and under the spell of this emotion Whitman turned out four elegies on the death of the President, all grouped in one edition of *Leaves of Grass* under the heading "President Lincoln's Burial Hymn." Of these, surely the best known is "O Captain! My Captain!" For a long time this lyric was regarded as *the* elegy for Lincoln and as Whitman's very best single poem as well. Sensitive readers today, especially with Whitman's "Lilacs" in mind, are not impressed. Many have spoken of how sentimental it is and of how uncharacteristic it is. Whitman himself later was embarrassed by it and almost wished he had never produced it. It is best to look upon it as a good poem, sincere if unrestrained, and suffering most because it stands in the shadow of the "Lilacs."

O CAPTAIN! MY CAPTAIN!

O Captain! my Captain! our fearful trip is done,
The ship has weather'd every rack, the prize we sought is
    won,
The port is near, the bells I hear, the people all exulting,
While follow eyes the steady keel, the vessel grim and
    daring;
        But O heart! heart! heart!
            O the bleeding drops of red,
                Where on the deck my Captain lies,
                    Fallen cold and dead.

O Captain! my Captain! rise up and hear the bells;
Rise up—for you the flag is flung—for you the bugle trills,
For you bouquets and ribbon'd wreaths—for you the shores
    a-crowding,
For you they call, the swaying mass, their eager faces turning;
        Here Captain! dear father!
        The arm beneath your head!
        It is some dream that on the deck,
            You've fallen cold and dead.

My Captain does not answer, his lips are pale and still,
My father does not feel my arm, he has no pulse nor will,
The ship is anchor'd safe and sound, its voyage closed and
    done,
From fearful trip the victor ship comes in with object won;
        Exult O shores, and ring O bells!
        But I with mournful tread,
        Walk the deck my Captain lies,
            Fallen cold and dead.

When *Lilacs Last in the Dooryard Bloom'd* is, almost
everyone would acknowledge, America's most beautiful
elegy. Its inspiration is a noble figure and its theme is nobly
executed. As early as 1885 Stedman gave it this high place:
"The burial hymn, 'When Lilacs last,' etc., is entitled to the
repute in which it is affectionately held. The theme is
handled in an indirect, melodious, pathetic manner, and I
think this poem and Lowell's 'Commemoration Ode,' each
in its own way, the most notable elegies resulting from the
war and its episodes. Whitman's is exquisitely idyllic,
Lowell's the more heroic and intellectual."

Three symbols function through the poem to give form
to the poet's very complex emotional state. The first is the
western star, which clearly stands for the fallen President;
the second is the lilac, with its heart-shaped leaves of rich

green, which apparently represents the poet's love for his subject; the third is the solitary thrush, singing from secluded recesses, which may be taken as the poet himself, caroling a song, first of grief and then of joy. Or another way to regard the symbols is to think of the western star as representing the mortal Lincoln, and the lilac blooming perennial as representing the immortal Lincoln, with again the thrush representing the poet in his song inspired by these two reflections. The Easter atmosphere in which Lincoln was shot and buried is thus powerfully appropriate. And most impressive, too, is the image of lines 120–122, where the poet pictures himself close-walking between two companions, the knowledge of death (reflection on the fact of mortality, which gives rise to grief) and the thought of death (confidence in Lincoln's immortality, which gives rise to joy).

The conflict is thus between two powerful and essentially opposite emotions. Lincoln is dead, and for this loss we grieve; but the lilac with its heart-shaped leaves of rich green blooms perennial, and for this we burst with joy.

WHEN LILACS LAST IN THE DOORYARD BLOOM'D

1

When lilacs last in the dooryard bloom'd,
And the great star early droop'd in the western sky in the
    night,
I mourn'd, and yet shall mourn with ever-returning spring.

Ever-returning spring, trinity sure to me you bring,
Lilac blooming perennial and drooping star in the west,
And thought of him I love.

2

O powerful western fallen star!
O shades of night—O moody, tearful night!
O great star disappear'd—O the black murk that hides
the star!
O cruel hands that hold me powerless—O helpless soul
of me!
O harsh surrounding cloud that will not free my soul.

3

In the dooryard fronting an old farm-house near the white-
wash'd palings,
Stands the lilac-bush tall-growing with heart-shaped leaves
of rich green,
With many a pointed blossom rising delicate, with the
perfume strong I love,
With every leaf a miracle—and from this bush in the
dooryard,
With delicate-color'd blossoms and heart-shaped leaves
of rich green,
A sprig with its flower I break.

4

In the swamp in secluded recesses,
A shy and hidden bird is warbling a song.

Solitary the thrush,
The hermit withdrawn to himself, avoiding the settlements,
Sings by himself a song.

Song of the bleeding throat,
Death's outlet song of life, (for well dear brother I know,
If thou wast not granted to sing thou woulds't surely die.)

5

Over the breast of the spring, the land, amid cities,
Amid lanes and through old woods, where lately the violets
    peep'd from the ground, spotting the gray débris,
Amid the grass in the fields each side of the lanes, passing
    the endless grass,
Passing the yellow-spear'd wheat, every grain from its shroud
    in the dark-brown fields uprisen,
Passing the apple-tree blows of white and pink in the
    orchards,
Carrying a corpse to where it shall rest in the grave,
Night and day journeys a coffin.

6

Coffin that passes through lanes and streets,
Through day and night with the great cloud darkening
    the land,
With the pomp of the inloop'd flags with the cities draped
    in black,
With the show of the States themselves as of crape-veil'd
    women standing,
With processions long and winding and the flambeaus of
    the night,
With the countless torches lit, with the silent sea of faces
    and the unbared heads,
With the waiting depot, the arriving coffin, and the somber
    faces,
With dirges through the night, with the thousand voices
    rising strong and solemn,
With all the mournful voices of the dirges pour'd around
    the coffin,
The dim-lit churches and the shuddering organs—where
    amid these you journey,

With the tolling tolling bells' perpetual clang,
Here, coffin that slowly passes,
I give you my sprig of lilac.

7

(Nor for you, for one alone,
Blossoms and branches green to coffins all I bring,
For fresh as the morning, thus would I chant a song for you
   O sane and sacred death.

All over bouquets of roses,
O death, I cover you over with roses and early lilies,
But mostly and now the lilac that blooms the first,
Copious I break, I break the sprigs from the bushes,
With loaded arms I come, pouring for you,
For you and the coffins all of you O death.)

8

O western orb sailing the heaven,
Now I know what you must have meant as a month since
   I walk'd,
As I walk'd in silence the transparent shadowy night,
As I saw you had something to tell as you bent to me night
   after night,
As you droop'd from the sky low down as if to my side,
   (while the other stars all look'd on,)
As we wander'd together the solemn night, (for something
   I know not what kept me from sleep,)
As the night advanced, and I saw on the rim of the west
   how full you were of woe,
As I stood on the rising ground in the breeze in the cool
   transparent night,
As I watch'd where you pass'd and was lost in the nether-
   ward black of the night,

As my soul in its trouble dissatisfied sank, as where you
    sad orb,
Concluded, dropt in the night, and was gone.

9

Sing on there in the swamp,
O singer bashful and tender, I hear your notes, I hear
    your call,
I hear, I come presently, I understand you,
But a moment I linger, for the lustrous star has detain'd
    me,
The star my departing comrade holds and detains me.

10

O how shall I warble myself for the dead one there I loved?
And how shall I deck my song for the large sweet soul that
    has gone?
And what shall my perfume be for the grave of him I love?

Sea-winds blown from east and west,
Blown from the Eastern sea and blown from the Western
    sea, till there on the prairies meeting,
These and with these and the breath of my chant,
I'll perfume the grave of him I love.

11

O what shall I hang on the chamber walls?
And what shall the pictures be that I hang on the walls,
To adorn the burial-house of him I love?

Pictures of growing spring and farms and homes,
With the Fourth-month eve at sundown, and the gray
    smoke lucid and bright,

With floods of the yellow gold of the gorgeous, indolent,
   sinking sun, burning, expanding the air,
With the fresh sweet herbage under foot, and the pale
   green leaves of the trees prolific,
In the distance the flowing glaze, the breast of the river,
   with a wind-dapple here and there,
With ranging hills on the banks, with many a line against
   the sky, and shadows,
And the city at hand, with dwellings so dense, and stacks
   of chimneys,
And all the scenes of life and the workshops, and the
   workmen homeward returning.

12

Lo, body and soul—this land,
My own Manhattan with spires, and the sparkling and
   hurrying tides, and the ships,
The varied and ample land, the South and the North in
   the light, Ohio's shores and flashing Missouri,
And ever the far-spreading prairies cover'd with grass and
   corn.

Lo, the most excellent sun so calm and haughty,
The violet and purple morn with just-felt breezes,
The gentle soft-born measureless light,
The miracle spreading bathing all, the fulfill'd noon,
The coming eve delicious, the welcome night and the stars,
Over my cities shining all, enveloping man and land.

13

Sing on, sing on you gray-brown bird,
Sing from the swamps, the recesses, pour your chant from
   the bushes,

Limitless out of the dusk, out of the cedars and pines.
Sing on dearest brother, warble your reedy song,
Loud human song, with voice of uttermost woe.

O liquid and free and tender!
O wild and loose to my soul—O wondrous singer!
You only I hear—yet the star holds me, (but will soon
  depart,)
Yet the lilac with mastering odor holds me.

14

Now while I sat in the day and look'd forth,
In the close of the day with its light and the fields of
  spring, and the farmers preparing their crops,
In the large unconscious scenery of my land with its lakes
  and forests,
In the heavenly aerial beauty, (after the perturb'd winds
  and the storms,)
Under the arching heavens of the afternoon swift passing,
  and the voices of children and women,
The many-moving sea-tides, and I saw the ships how they
  sail'd,
And the summer approaching with richness, and the fields
  all busy with labor,
And the infinite separate houses, how they all went on,
  each with its meals and minutia of daily usages,
And the streets how their throbbings throbb'd, and the
  cities pent—lo, then and there,
Falling upon them all and among them all, enveloping
  me with the rest,
Appear'd the cloud, appear'd the long black trail,
And I knew death, its thought, and the sacred knowledge
  of death.

Then with the knowledge of death as walking one side
   of me,
And the thought of death close-walking the other side of me,
And I in the middle as with companions, and as holding the
   hands of companions,
I fled forth to the hiding receiving night that talks not,
Down to the shores of the water, the path by the swamp in
   the dimness,
To the solemn shadowy cedars and ghostly pines so still.

And the singer so shy to the rest receiv'd me,
The gray-brown bird I know receiv'd us comrades three,
And he sang the carol of death, and a verse for him I love.

From deep secluded recesses,
From the fragrant cedars and the ghostly pines so still,
Came the carol of the bird.

And the charm of the carol rapt me
As I held as if by their hands my comrades in the night,
And the voice of my spirit tallied the song of the bird.

Come lovely and soothing death,
Undulate round the world, serenely arriving, arriving,
In the day, in the night, to all, to each,
Sooner or later delicate death.

Prais'd be the fathomless universe,
For life and joy, and for objects and knowledge curious,
And for love, sweet love—but praise! praise! praise!
For the sure-enwinding arms of cool-enfolding death.

Dark mother always gliding near with soft feet,
Have none chanted for thee a chant of fullest welcome?
Then I chant it for thee, I glorify thee above all,
I bring thee a song that when thou must indeed come, come
   unfalteringly.

Approach strong deliveress,
When it is so, when thou hast taken them I joyously sing
    the dead,
Lost in the loving floating ocean of thee,
Laved in the flood of thy bliss O death.

From me to thee glad serenades,
Dances for thee I propose saluting thee, adornments and
    feastings for thee,
And the sights of the open landscape and the high-spread
    sky are fitting,
And life and the fields, and the huge and thoughtful night.

The night in silence under many a star,
The ocean shore and the husky whispering wave whose
    voice I know,
And the soul turning to thee O vast and well-veil'd death,
And the body gratefully nestling close to thee.

Over the tree-tops I float thee a song,
Over the rising and sinking waves, over the myriad fields
    and the prairies wide,
Over the dense-pack'd cities all and the teeming wharves
    and ways,
I float this carol with joy, with joy to thee O death.

15

To the tally of my soul,
Loud and strong kept up the gray-brown bird,
With pure deliberate notes spreading filling the night.

Loud in the pines and cedars dim,
Clear in the freshness moist and the swamp-perfume,
And I with my comrades there in the night.

While my sight that was bound in my eyes unclosed,
As to long panoramas of visions.

And I saw askant the armies,
I saw as in noiseless dreams hundreds of battle-flags,
Borne through the smoke of the battles and pierc'd with
    missiles I saw them,
And carried hither and yon through the smoke, and torn
    and bloody,
And at last but a few shreds left on the staffs, (and all
    in silence,)
And the staffs all splinter'd and broken.

I saw battle-corpses, myriads of them,
And the white skeletons of young men, I saw them,
I saw the débris and débris of all the slain soldiers of the war,
But I saw they were not as was thought,
They themselves were fully at rest, they suffer'd not,
The living remain'd and suffer'd, the mother suffer'd,
And the wife and the child and the musing comrade suffer'd,
And the armies that remain'd suffer'd.

16

Passing the visions, passing the night,
Passing, unloosing the hold of my comrades' hands,
Passing the song of the hermit bird and the tallying song
    of my soul,
Victorious song, death's outlet song, yet varying ever-
    altering song,
As low and wailing, yet clear the notes, rising and falling,
    flooding the night,
Sadly sinking and fainting, as warning and warning, and
    yet again bursting with joy,
Covering the earth and filling the spread of the heaven,
As that powerful psalm in the night I heard from recesses,
Passing, I leave thee lilac with heart-shaped leaves,
I leave thee there in the dooryard, blooming, returning
    with spring.

I cease from my song for thee,
From my gaze on thee in the west, fronting the west,
    communing with thee,
O comrade lustrous with silver face in the night.

Yet each to keep and all, retrievements out of the night,
The song, the wondrous chant of the gray-brown bird,
And the tallying chant, the echo arous'd in my soul,
With the lustrous and drooping star with the countenance
    full of woe,
With the holders holding my hand nearing the call of the
    bird,
Comrades mine and *I* in the midst, and their memory ever
    to keep, for the dead *I* loved so well,
For the sweetest, wisest soul of all my days and lands—and
    this for his dear sake,
Lilac and star and bird twined with the chant of my soul,
There in the fragrant pines and the cedars dusk and dim.

The tiny lyric "Hush'd Be the Camps To-day" poignantly
renders the grief of the soldiers for their Commander-
in-Chief.

HUSH'D BE THE CAMPS TO-DAY

(May 4, 1865)

Hush'd be the camps to-day,
And soldiers let us drape our war-worn weapons,
And each with musing soul retire to celebrate,
Our dear commander's death.

No more for him life's stormy conflicts,
Nor victory, nor defeat—no more time's dark events,
Charging like ceaseless clouds across the sky.

But sing poet in our name,
Sing of the love we bore him—because you, dweller in
  camps, know it truly.

As they invault the coffin there,
Sing—as they close the doors of earth upon him—one verse,
For the heavy hearts of soldiers.

In "This Dust Was Once the Man" the poet refers to the assassination as the "foulest crime in history" and credits Lincoln with the saving of the United States.

THIS DUST WAS ONCE THE MAN

This dust was once the man,
Gentle, plain, just and resolute, under whose cautious hand,
Against the foulest crime in history known in any land or
  age,
Was saved the Union of these States.

Herman Melville

1819–1891

ALTHOUGH there is no way now to know how much he may have been impressed, if at all, Lincoln did on one occasion meet the author of *Moby Dick*.

Too late for the formal inauguration of the new president, but in time for the second grand reception, Herman Melville, at the instigation of his brother Allan and encouraged by the vigorous support of the citizens of Pittsfield, Massachusetts, journeyed by way of Albany and New York to Washington to secure appointment as consul to Florence. Though he failed to win the appointment, Melville apparently enjoyed his evening at the White House. He describes the inaugural festivities in a letter to his wife Elizabeth on the succeeding Sunday afternoon, late in March, only two weeks before the firing on Fort Sumter:

There was a great crowd, and a brilliant scene. Ladies in full dress by the hundred. A steady stream of two-and-twos wound thro' the apartments shaking hands with "Old Abe" and immediately passing on. This continued without cessation for an hour and a half. Of course I was one of the shakers. Old Abe is much better looking than I expected and younger looking. He shook hands like a good fellow—working hard at it like a man sawing wood at so much per cord. Mrs. Lincoln is rather good-looking I thought. The scene was very fine altogether. Superb furniture—flood of light—magnificent flowers—full band of music, etc.

When Fort Sumter was attacked on April 12, and the President three days later called for 75,000 volunteers,

Melville's name promptly appeared on the militia roll in Pittsfield. He was never actually to serve in the war, but he did regularly visit the war camps at the front. He felt the war intensely and the news of Lee's surrender at Appomattox Court House he received with relief and joy.

Six days later there came the news of the assassination, and, like so many others, he felt his relief chilled to stone. His sensations, which he, probably quite properly, ascribes to the People, he later set down in "The Martyr." The feeling here is one of intense sorrow, but throbbing through it is the heavy claim of Vengeance. The lyric, one of Melville's best poems, is distinguished by a most impressive employment of muffled refrain.

THE MARTYR

*Indicative of the Passion of the People
on the 15th Day of April, 1865*

Good Friday was the day
  Of the prodigy and crime,
When they killed him in his pity,
  When they killed him in his prime
Of clemency and calm—
    When with yearning he was filled
    To redeem the evil-willed,
And, though conqueror, be kind;
  But they killed him in his kindness,
  In their madness and their blindness,
And they killed him from behind.

There is sobbing of the strong,
  And a pall upon the land;
But the People in their weeping
  Bare the iron hand:

Beware the People weeping
When they bare the iron hand.

He lieth in his blood—
The father in his face;
They have killed him, the Forgiver—
The Avenger takes his place,
The Avenger wisely stern,
Who in righteousness shall do
What the heavens call him to,
And the parricides remand;
For they killed him in his kindness,
In their madness and their blindness,
And his blood is on their hand.

There is sobbing of the strong,
And a pall upon the land;
But the People in their weeping
Bare the iron hand:
Beware the People weeping
When they bare the iron hand.

Edward Rowland Sill

1841–1887

Like James Whitcomb Riley, Edward Rowland Sill was just a young man at the time of the Civil War. And he was yet a young man, just twenty-four, when at the war's end he composed his long poem *Man, the Spirit*, which includes a lyrical elegy to Lincoln.

Alfred Riggs Ferguson, writing of Sill in *The Twilight Poet*, remarks on the reception accorded *Man, the Spirit*. He explains that a German critic had singled out the poem as "an example of American vitality in literature." But the critic, much impressed by the vividness of the Lincoln lyric, was so afraid that the beauty of the elegy would be lost in translation that he reprinted it in English for his German readers. The Lincoln section, now entitled "The Noblest Soul of All," was reprinted shortly after by the *London Reader*, which had been led to it through the German review. Here the budding poet was described as one "whose name will certainly ere long become familiar to all true lovers of poetry." Almost exactly one year after the day of the assassination the poem was published again, this time in Littell's *Living Age*, an American magazine.

With its simple diction and formal structure, the elegy is in the style later to be so characteristic of the California professor-poet. Despite its obvious warmth, it may seem a little prosaic to us today. Perhaps in its last two stanzas the true voice of the poet can be heard.

THE DEAD PRESIDENT

Were there no crowns on earth,
No evergreen to weave a hero's wreath,
That he must pass beyond the gates of death,
Our hero, our slain hero, to be crowned?
Could there on our unworthy earth be found
    Naught to befit his worth?

The noblest soul of all!
When was there ever, since our Washington,
A man so pure, so wise, so patient—one
Who walked with this high goal alone in sight,
To speak, to do, to sanction only Right,
    Though very heaven should fall!

Ah, not for him we weep;
What honor more could be in store for him?
And troublesome world, when his great work was done?
Who would have had him linger in our dim
Who would not leave that worn and weary one
    Gladly to go to sleep?

For us the stroke was just;
We were not worthy of that patient heart;
We might have helped him more, not stood apart,
And coldly criticised his works and ways—
Too late now, all too late—our little praise
    Sounds hollow o'er his dust.

Be merciful, O our God!
Forgive the meanness of our human hearts,
That never, till a noble soul departs,
See half the worth, or hear the angel's wings
Till they go rustling heavenward as he springs
    Up from the mounded sod.

Yet what a deathless crown
Of Northern pine and Southern orange-flower,
For victory, and the land's new bridal hour,
Would we have wreathed for that beloved brow!
Sadly upon his sleeping forehead now
    We lay our cypress down.

O martyred one, farewell!
Thou hast not left thy people quite alone,
Out of thy beautiful life there comes a tone
Of power, of love, of trust, a prophecy,
Whose fair fulfillment all the earth shall be,
    And all the future tell.

James Whitcomb Riley
1849–1916

JAMES WHITCOMB RILEY is one of America's most homespun poets. That he should feel an affection and admiration for America's most homespun president is not
surprising. Once he remarked of the man who had been
President while he romped in the fields and swimming holes
of Hoosier Indiana: "The great Lincoln—the most perfect
American type, doubtless, in history . . . the high character of the man at once loved and revered of all nations
. . . a personage of such lofty genius and yet so simply
lovable."

At another time he testified to Lincoln's immense capacities: "Lincoln was a rich man. He lived in the American
woods. They said it was a mental wilderness. It was a
mental university. How rich he was with that handful of
seven books by the cabin fire. What value he attached to his
visit to this world, every day a day of discovery, a new survey
of facts and principles, every day reaching out like the
wide-spreading trees around him for soil and water."

Riley's father had been Indiana's Sixth District elector at
the Chicago convention that nominated Lincoln for the
Presidency. He had served through the war and was home
on furlough at the time of the assassination. The sixteen-
year-old boy, according to his biographer, heard his father a
few days later "deliver an eloquent tribute at a memorial
meeting for the assassinated President."

In his late years Riley was acclaimed the country over. He was revered as The Hoosier Poet and The Poet of Democracy. In 1915 his birthday was celebrated in Indiana as Riley Day, and on this gala occasion the *Christian Science Monitor* compared the poet to Lincoln: ". . . the same instruments—pathos, humor, and sincere love of men as men."

Riley produced two poems on Abraham Lincoln. The first, simply entitled "Lincoln," leads up to the now familiar identification of the President with Christ. It is a hymn to the peaceful existence that Riley loved and for which Lincoln surrendered his life.

LINCOLN

A peaceful life;—just toil and rest—
   All his desire;—
To read the books he liked the best
   Beside the cabin fire—
God's word and man's;—to peer sometimes
   Above the page, in smoldering gleams,
And catch, like far heroic rhymes,
   The on-march of his dreams.

A peaceful life;—to hear the low
   Of pastured herds,
Of woodman's ax that, blow on blow,
   Fell sweet as rhythmic words.
And yet there stirred within his breast
   A fateful pulse that, like a roll
Of drums, made high above his rest
   A tumult in his soul.

A peaceful life! . . . They haled him even
   As One was haled
Whose open palms were nailed toward Heaven

When prayers nor aught availed.
And, lo, he paid the selfsame price
To lull a nation's awful strife
And will us, through the sacrifice
Of self, his peaceful life.

The second, entitled "Lincoln—the Boy," is written in the Hoosier Poet's own inimitable style. It celebrates chiefly the sense of brotherhood so conspicuous in the life and character of Lincoln, as boy and as President.

LINCOLN—THE BOY

O simple as the rhymes that tell
The simplest tales of youth,
Or simple as a miracle
Beside the simplest truth—
So simple seems the view we share
With our Immortals, sheer
From Glory looking down to where
They were as children here.

Or thus we know, nor doubt it not,
The boy he must have been
Whose budding heart bloomed with the thought
All men are kith and kin—
With love-light in his eyes and shade
Of prescient tears:—Because
Only of such a boy were made
The loving man he was.

Edwin Markham

1852–1940

Edwin Markham was only a boy during the years the great war raged, and he was never to know the war firsthand or the President personally. But in his youth and later he heard vivid accounts of the battles and many tales of the martyred President. Eventually he came to know Abraham Lincoln so well that he felt he could write with authority on his character and on his place in history. On one occasion the poet of "The Man with the Hoe" penned a beautiful tribute to his greatness:

Lincoln was great not because he occupied the Presidential chair. The matter of importance is not the place a man fills, but how he fills it; not even the achievement of his life, but the spirit of his life. A man in public life, if he looks on his office as a mere instrument to give him power and glory, is only an empty shell. But if he keeps his petty ego suppressed and looks on his office as a fortunate instrument to enable him to serve the people, to establish justice, to increase good will, then his office becomes an altar of righteousness, a hiding-place of the Almighty. Lincoln belonged to the high order of men. . . . And now, in our own day, nearly seventy years after, Lincoln stands forth as the all-round man in our history, as the supreme man of the republic. . . . Yes, Lincoln went down in tragic death, but he is even greater in his death than he ever was in his life. For he has risen to become the national ideal, the great spiritual power kindling a great people.

This reverence for Lincoln was the inspiration for a number of poems at Markham's hand. Certainly the most

64

impressive of these, and the only poem of his which can rival the beauty of "The Man with the Hoe," is his "Lincoln, the Man of the People," written in Brooklyn in 1899, in response to a request.

Of this poem Markham's biographer William Stidger speaks with unreserved enthusiasm: "It is generally conceded by poets and critics alike that Markham's poem on Abraham Lincoln is the greatest utterance ever written on that great American martyr. It stands out as the Mount Everest of them all." He calls it "the greatest of thousands of Lincoln poems, . . . expressive of that individualistic philosophy of Edwin Markham." Among the poets and critics who have held the poem in the same esteem are Henry Van Dyke and Alfred Noyes. The former has observed: "Edwin Markham's 'Lincoln' is the greatest poem ever written on the immortal martyr, and the greatest that ever will be written." And Noyes once remarked of the concluding figure that it was "the most impressive climax in English poetry."

Stidger tells in great detail the story of the poem's inception as he had it from the poet himself. And quite a story it is. He quotes Markham:

"The call came at the end of 1899, at the end of the nineteenth century. Four grave and reverend seniors, from a rich, exclusive New York Club, knocked at my door in Brooklyn, my first home in the crowded East.

"I was told that their select company were about to have a Babylonian banquet at Delmonico's to celebrate the first Lincoln Birthday anniversary in the twentieth century. The rail-splitter whose early rations were slices of bacon and a hunk of corn bread was now to be honored with a groaning banquet table at twenty dollars a plate.

"Would I have the grace and good will to write a Lincoln poem for the memorable occasion? I was assured that I had been chosen by the club from all the living American poets for this illustrious honor.

"Yes, I would be glad to pay my homage to greatness. Yet I told my callers that I had to go out lecture-reading, and to take an eagle-swing over the Middle West. But I would meditate upon the poem all the way, and would return in time to give three weeks to the composition.

"I remember that I said: 'Gentlemen, for Lincoln I have deep love and reverence. I will wait patiently upon the Muse: if she gives the poem to me, I will give the poem to you. I cannot promise with certainty."

Stidger then, having spoken of Markham's early enthusiasm for the figure of Abraham Lincoln, in great detail reports the shaping of the poem in the poet's imagination. The story as we have it reminds us of the experience of James Russell Lowell in his writing of the "Ode."

But the poem was completed in time, and it was read at the Lincoln Birthday Dinner sponsored by the Republican Club of New York City in 1900.

It was this poem, too, Stidger reminds us, that was selected by a Congressional committee, headed by Chief Justice Taft, to be read as part of the dedication services in 1922 for the Lincoln Memorial, construction of which had begun on Lincoln's birthday, 1914. The President of the United States, Warren G. Harding, delivered the address, and the poet himself read the poem. According to Stidger, the service was "one of the first great broadcasts over the radio from Washington under government auspices, and while one hundred thousand people listened on the ground three million heard it over the radio."

The poem, like so many of the odes to the President, celebrates Lincoln's humility, the humility of a man who "faltered not at praise." Almost as popular as "The Man with the Hoe," his "Lincoln," like that other great lyric, is charged with the generous sympathy Markham felt for the common man. And certainly Alfred Noyes, in praising the poem for its lyrical beauty, has done right to refer us to the magnificent closing lines.

LINCOLN, THE MAN OF THE PEOPLE

When the Norn Mother saw the Whirlwind Hour
Greatening and darkening as it hurried on,
She left the Heaven of Heroes and came down
To make a man to meet the mortal need.
She took the tried clay of the common road—
Clay warm yet with the genial heat of earth,
Dasht through it all a strain of prophecy;
Tempered the heap with thrill of human tears;
Then mixt a laughter with the serious stuff.
Into the shape she breathed a flame to light
That tender, tragic, ever-changing face;
And laid on him a sense of the Mystic Powers,
Moving—all husht—behind the mortal veil.
Here was a man to hold against the world,
A man to match the mountains and the sea.

The color of the ground was in him, the red earth;
The smack and tang of elemental things:
The rectitude and patience of the cliff;
The good-will of the rain that loves all leaves;
The friendly welcome of the wayside well;
The courage of the bird that dares the sea;
The gladness of the wind that shakes the corn;
The pity of the snow that hides all scars;
The secrecy of streams that make their way
Under the mountain to the rifted rock;
The tolerance and equity of light
That gives as freely to the shrinking flower
As to the great oak flaring to the wind—
To the grave's low hill as to the Matterhorn

That shoulders out the sky. Sprung from the West,
He drank the valorous youth of a new world.
The strength of virgin forests braced his mind,
The hush of spacious prairies stilled his soul.
His words were oaks in acorns; and his thoughts
Were roots that firmly gript the granite truth.

Up from log cabin to the Capitol,
One fire was on his spirit, one resolve—
To send the keen ax to the root of wrong,
Clearing a free way for the feet of God,
The eyes of conscience testing every stroke,
To make his deed the measure of a man.
He built the rail-pile as he built the State,
Pouring his splendid strength through every blow:
The grip that swung the ax in Illinois
Was on the pen that set a people free.

So came the Captain with the mighty heart.
And when the judgment thunders split the house,
Wrenching the rafters from their ancient rest,
He held the ridgepole up, and spiked again
The rafters of the Home. He held his place—
Held the long purpose like a growing tree—
Held on through blame and faltered not at praise.
And when he fell in whirlwind, he went down
As when a lordly cedar, green with boughs,
Goes down with a great shout upon the hills,
And leaves a lonesome place against the sky.

Among the other Lincoln lyrics composed by Markham
three are especially notable: "Young Lincoln," "Lincoln
Slain," and "Lincoln Triumphant." The first records the
early life of Lincoln in order to account for the character of
the President. It shows his only fault to be a virtue.

YOUNG LINCOLN

Men saw no portents on that winter night
A hundred years ago. No omens flared
Above that trail-watched cabin with one door,
And windowless to all the peering stars.
They laid him in the hollow of a log,
Humblest of cradles, save that other one—
The manger in the stall at Bethlehem.

No portents! Yet with whisper and alarm
The Evil Powers that dread the nearing feet
Of heroes, held a council in that hour;
And sent three fates to darken that low door,
To baffle and beat back the heaven-sent child.
Three were the fates—gaunt Poverty that chains,
Gray Drudgery that grinds the hope away,
And gaping Ignorance that starves the soul.

They came with secret laughters to destroy.
Ever they dogged him, counting every step,
Waylaid his youth and struggled for his soul.
They came to master but he made them serve;
And from the wrestle with the destinies,
He rose with all his energies aglow.
For God upon whose steadfast shoulders rest
These governments of ours, had not forgot.
He needed for his purposes a voice,
A voice to be a clarion on the wind,
Crying the word of freedom to dead hearts,
The word that centuries had waited for.

So hidden in the West, God shaped his man.
There in the unspoiled solitude he grew,
Unwarped by culture and uncramped by creed;

Keeping his course courageous and alone,
As goes the Mississippi to the sea.
His daring spirit burst the narrow bounds,
Rose resolute; and like the sea-called stream,
He tore new channels where he found no way.
His tools were his first teachers, sternly kind.
The plow, the scythe, the maul, the echoing ax
Taught him their homely wisdom and their peace.
He had the plain man's genius—common sense;
Yet rage for knowledge drove his mind afar;
He fed his spirit with the bread of books,
And slaked his thirst at all the wells of thought.

But most he read the heart of common man,
Scanned all its secret pages stained with tears,
Saw all the guile, saw all the piteous pain;
And yet could keep the smile above his lips,
Love and forgive, see all and pardon all;
His only fault, the fault that some of old
Laid even on God—that he was even wont
To bend the law to let his mercy out.

Technically interesting is the little lyric "Lincoln Slain."
It will be noted that the basic meter of the poem is trochaic
tetrameter; but a most effective variation is introduced in
the third line of each stanza, each of which begins with an
easy anapest. Another impressive variation figures in the
unique rhyme scheme. While the end sound of the first line
for each stanza is never echoed, the second line is made to
rhyme in a strong masculine single syllable with the fifth;
and, by contrast, the third and fourth lines depend upon a
feminine rhyme. The poet by means of these variations and
contrasts is able to make more impressive his theme, which
is defined in the word *but* in the poem and has to do with
the conflict in emotion felt by a nation at once grief-

stricken and grateful. Besides, the last line of each stanza
not only requires a slow, deliberate reading because of its
meter and syllable spacing, but is made heavy with the long
o sound, and emphatic through repetition. All in all, the
poem is rich in lyrical effects appropriate to the desired tone
and mood.

Here are the lilacs and the thrushes again. The poet
insists that as consolation for their grief the people have the
sense they are *one* people.

LINCOLN SLAIN

In the moment of his glory,
Treason strikes the leader down;
And a wail of lamentation
Sweeps across the mourning nation,
Road to road and town to town.

Dead he lies, the great beloved,
Dead the captain in command;
And the cries of desolation
Moan across the martyred nation,
Moan across a lonely land.

Husht are April's singing thrushes,
And her lilacs flaunt no more;
But the people are one people
In the knell from tower and steeple,
In the grief from shore to shore.

Perhaps Markham's much anthologized "Lincoln Triumphant" is excessively sentimental. And certainly the lyric
is not so interesting as "Lincoln Slain." But here Abraham
Lincoln is seen triumphant over death, in his immortality
leading an energetic nation forward toward an ideal of

brotherhood. The image with which the poem closes is not without effect, and doubtless it will remind some readers of the figure with which Gerard Manley Hopkins closes his sonnet "God's Grandeur."

LINCOLN TRIUMPHANT

Lincoln is not dead. He lives
In all that pities and forgives.
He has arisen and sheds a fire
That makes America aspire.

Even now as, when in life, he led,
He leads us onward from the dead;
Yes, over the whole wide world he bends
To make the world a world of friends.

Edwin Arlington Robinson
1869–1935

I T was perfectly natural that E. A. Robinson, with his generous social sympathy and his concern for the political situation, should pay his respects in verse to the memory of Abraham Lincoln. Robinson, whose home in Gardiner, Maine, was on Lincoln Street, had been disappointed in the failure of William Jennings Bryan to defeat William McKinley in the election of 1896. Robinson held Bryan, perhaps in part because of his passionate rhetoric, in the highest esteem, in fact revered him as the greatest political figure in America since Lincoln.

But his enthusiasm for the vice-president and McKinley's successor is well known. It was Theodore Roosevelt who had "discovered" Robinson through his reading of *The Children of the Night*, which his fourteen-year-old son Kermit had placed in his hands. One of Kermit's instructors at Groton was Henry Richards, Jr., of Gardiner, and when the boy solicited some special advice on reading his teacher let him have *The Children of the Night*. The youngster was so much impressed that he ordered copies from the Badger publishing house, and on January 19, 1904, sent one to his father. In the fall of that year as he finished out McKinley's term and campaigned for re-election the President read the poetry of the obscure subway worker.

Later it was to Kermit that the poet sent the manuscript of the poem "The Man Who Came," afterwards entitled

"The Master." And Robinson's biographer, Hermann Hagedorn (who himself produced a Lincoln elegy, "Oh, Patient Eyes"), tells us that Henry Cabot Lodge, senator from Massachusetts, read the poem on Lincoln aloud to the family assembled in the White House.

The poem is not sentimental, but it is not without feeling either, a feeling that is warm and genuine. Robinson had a marvelous facility, even when pondering the pitiful lives of Eben Flood and Reuben Bright and Bewick Finzer, to stand off, to objectify his emotion. In such poems his touch and taste were perfect. And they are here. It is a lyric that is stamped indelibly "E. A. Robinson."

The poem does a number of things. Historically, it reflects the changes in attitude experienced by people close to Lincoln, such changes as we have already seen reflected in the remarks of James Russell Lowell and William Cullen Bryant. For Robinson's own time the poem can be read as a sharp commentary on the ugly commercialism then rampant. But chiefly "The Master" places Abraham Lincoln among the heroes of Thomas Carlyle, as a man who came forth in a time of crisis to direct history. Robinson credits Lincoln with saving the nation. And, as Lincoln saved the nation then, perhaps his resurrected spirit will do it now.

"The Master" is a sublime lyric.

THE MASTER

(Lincoln. Supposed to have been written
not long after the Civil War)

*A flying word from here and there
Had sown the name at which we sneered,
But soon the name was everywhere,
To be reviled and then revered:*

A presence to be loved and feared,
We cannot hide it, or deny
That we, the gentlemen who jeered,
May be forgotten by and by.

He came when days were perilous
And hearts of men were sore beguiled;
And having made his note of us,
He pondered and was reconciled.
Was ever master yet so mild
As he, and so untamable?
We doubted, even when he smiled,
Not knowing what he knew so well.

He knew that undeceiving fate
Would shame us whom he served unsought;
He knew that he must wince and wait—
The jest of those for whom he fought;
He knew devoutly what he thought
Of us and of our ridicule;
He knew that we must all be taught
Like little children in a school.

We gave a glamour to the task
That he encountered and saw through,
But little of us did he ask,
And little did we ever do.
And what appears if we review
The season when we railed and chaffed?
It is the face of one who knew
That we were learning while we laughed.

The face that in our vision feels
Again the venom that we flung,
Transfigured to the world reveals
The vigilance to which we clung.
Shrewd, hallowed, harassed, and among

The mysteries that are untold,
The face we see was never young,
Nor could it ever have been old.

For he, to whom we had applied
Our shopman's test of age and worth,
Was elemental when he died,
As he was ancient at his birth:
The saddest among kings of earth,
Bowed with a galling crown, this man
Met rancor with a cryptic mirth,
Laconic—and Olympian.

The love, the grandeur, and the fame
Are bounded by the world alone;
The calm, the smoldering, and the flame
Of awful patience were his own:
With him they are forever flown
Past all our fond self-shadowings,
Wherewith we cumber the Unknown
As with inept Icarian wings.

For we were not as other men:
'Twas ours to soar and his to see.
But we are coming down again,
And we shall come down pleasantly;
Nor shall we longer disagree
On what it is to be sublime,
But flourish in our perigee
And have one Titan at a time.

Frederic Ridgely Torrence
1875–1950

O NE of E. A. Robinson's closest friends and later the editor of the poet's letters, Ridgely Torrence, also produced an accomplished poem on the subject of Lincoln. A playwright as well as poet, Torrence was really the first to write plays of and for the American Negro. He has done more probably than any other single person to admit the Negro to the American theater, as actor and as subject. Notable among his *Plays for a Negro Theater* (1919) are *Granny Maumee, The Rider of Dreams,* and *Simon the Cyrenian*. For the sixteenth president of the United States, who had emancipated the slaves, Torrence's affections were strong.

In "Lincoln's Dream," a blank verse dramatic monologue, he credits to Lincoln's visionary power the capacity to foresee his violent death, and he picks up Whitman's metaphor to show the Ship of State in troubled waters.

LINCOLN'S DREAM

Before dawn, Good Friday, April 14th, 1865

How can I tell them what it was I saw
When none of them were with me in that world?
I was alone and always am alone.

No one from earth was with me in the dream,
On the dark ship again tonight bound outward.
Or in that other dream twelve nights ago
When, with the peace assured, I slept at last,
Then seemed to wake, roused by the sound of mourning
Here in the White House, and to find it empty,
To meet with no one that the eye could see
As I went searching, till I reached a thing
Not to be shared with others till its hour.
There in the East Room, waiting, there it was:
The mourners and the silence and the soldiers.
The unearthly funeral light that blazed from nowhere.
The high-raised catafalque. The Form that lay there
With the face covered. Hid. But not from me.
I knew it. Who knew better? There I lay.
"The President is dead." No need to say so.
Though the loud burst of grief that swept the dream
Moved me to want to tell it. But to whom?
Who, of the multitudes that walk in daylight,
Has understood when I have told my dreams?
They lack the gift or curse of having eyes
Or visions such as mine, that I had always,
Bloody presentments, shapes of fear and doom
That seemed to hint my kinship with the shades,
Even as a baby, staring through the chinks
At the red mists between me and the stars.
—"Bawn to see evil," old black Sam would say.

And afterwards, before I learned to read,
The grandeurs and the glooms that came about
When fever burned the veils before me thinner . . .
The cities seen before I ever reached them . . .
The worlds and faces boiling up from darkness
At night, in mother's time . . . "There, who's that,
    mother?

What's the man saying?" "What man?" "With the dagger."
"Why, Abe, there's no one there. You're seeing ghosts."
And so I was. And I have seen them since
And not less real than anything on earth
Seen with the outward eye lighted by reason.
We pioneers are superstitious people;
We live so near the edge of the unknown.
Though, if we see too much there, we can always
Look outward and fall back on common sense.
The line's as narrow as a razor edge
Between a mind well lighted and the darkness.
But what I've seen, I've seen. High noon's no clearer.
Daylight has yielded sight, as well as darkness.
For I was broad awake when I saw plain
My double image in the glass at Springfield,
One face alive, the other—not the same,
A thing to turn away from as I did.
And both reflected me. I knew its meaning:
The living face foretold my four years here,
The other—what's to come. I shudder at it,
But never for myself.

                    There's something else.
I've worn through every fear now but the worst,
Only to find it growing in my sleep,
Shaped in the vision of the shadowy ship.
Ten times I've dreamed it and again tonight,
Even in my broken rest, finding myself
Once more on board that dim, mysterious deck,
Fixed like a part of it and sensing only
Darkness, the hid wheel and the helmsman hidden
And prow set into darkness as the ship
Moves with a giant force through the dark water,
Swift to an unknown shore. And by what sea?
What is the ship? What passengers, what cargoes

Are gathered in that hold? I guess and fear
The portent, that the vessel in the dream
May be the brave and danger-blind republic
Marked for a further grief soon to be suffered.
What if some new blow threatens her and the dream
Comes as a sad foretelling? This may be.
I see it always like a shadow cast
Before some great event. And though it often
Presages some right triumph, yet not always.
For it appeared before our victories,
Antietam, Gettysburg,—but in the end
What did those victories cost us? Young men dead.
Dead. On both sides. The nation's life. The flower.
And in a war that never would have been
But for the blind pilots long before it struck.
So with all wars; there never yet was one
That might not, with clear vision and just action,
Have been avoided and the storm dissolved.
Yes, the republic lives. But for how long?
How long will she pursue through darkening seas
The free, unfearing course her builders laid?
What sorrows wait for her beyond the sea line?
What hidden shoals? What perils of the shallows?
Or from the bottom when the earthquakes come
Pushing up peaks with fangs unknown before?
Will she go down? Or some earth-rocking wave
Wash her free glories on yon shores, to lie
Manacled on the rocks, bare to the keel
That should have kept home harbor in the storm?
Or will she ride the deluge and then drift
Slowly to some Sargasso and lie there
And in the fat backwaters grope for comfort
Through the dry rot of never setting sail,
Rusting in fears, tangled in idle calms,
Never to dare new seas or hardier ways?

But beyond all that threatens, all that strikes,
Whatever shadows, bolts, disasters, dooms
Loom from the sea or air to bring her down,
None are so dangerous as those within,
Nursed in her freedom, suffered to be here,
A thousand evils, that we may be free
Of the one greater which would make us slaves.
So it will be with every state that sails
True to the free and democratic course;
The hardest of all paths to steer upon,
The easiest assailed, yet, in the end,
The only forward track. Which, being lost,
Must then, however late, be found and followed
And all begun again. Though dangers ride
Aboard this nation, she has carried danger
Since first the seas embraced her and she stood
Free to whatever winds the sky could send,
And sailed, as now, with hazards that could sink her.
With the self-seekers and the backward-turners
Who fought to shape her course as in these days.
With folly-chosen captains, then as now,
Swayed by the brainless will of those who place them.
With wrongs, with pilots who would sail astray
And with blind borers hollowing out the frame.
With blazing envies, hatreds that may spread
And with their sea-fires burn her to the ocean.
All these she carries and is still afloat.
I trust the people as I trust the stars.
And if they lose the reckoning they will find it,
For they must learn and by their griefs they will,
Must learn to steer themselves, steer or be steered.
And if they lose their freedom they will find it
And, lost for times enough, they'll learn to keep it.
They've come this far and they have weathered all
But what's to come.

Or is the vision larger
And the dark ship the earth, or life itself?
If so, these fears will have an end at last,
One with the breast that held them, as the vessel
Gathers my littleness and all its pain
Into that hold that bore me to this place
And with dark pointing takes me away again,
Perhaps to further shores or to some vastness
Where there may still be dawns or perhaps darkness.
But beyond that, there may be other dreams.

Is that you, John? I'm waiting for a message.
You're up too late, or early. Night's for sleep.
Boy, go lie down. I'll watch. It's not yet day.

Paul Laurence Dunbar

1872–1906

BOTH of the parents of Paul Dunbar had been slaves. And Lincoln they regarded as chiefly responsible for their emancipation. The boy grew up in an Ohio home where the assassinated President was always spoken of with reverence, and the picture of him that hung in the house was a constant reminder to them all that their freedom they owed to this man.

The poet, who all his short life wrote of and for his people, in his "Lincoln" looks upon the President as the healer of a mighty wound. He is the eternal hero called up by crisis as a sacrifice to destiny. He is written down among the treasured few.

LINCOLN

Hurt was the Nation with a mighty wound,
And all her ways were filled with clam'rous sound.
Wailed loud the South with unremitting grief,
And wept the North that could not find relief.
Then madness joined its harshest tone to strife:
A minor note swelled in the song of life
Till, stirring with the love that filled his breast,
But still, unflinching at the Right's behest
Grave Lincoln came, strong-handed from afar,—

The mighty Homer of the lyre of war!
'Twas he who bade the raging tempest cease,
Wrenched from his strings the harmony of peace,
Muted the strings that made the discord,—Wrong,
And gave his spirit up in thund'rous song.
Oh, mighty Master of the mighty lyre!
Earth heard and trembled at thy strains of fire:
Earth learned of thee what Heaven already knew,
And wrote thee down among her treasured few!

Harriet Monroe
1860–1936

H ARRIET MONROE was born in Chicago just before the outbreak of the Civil War. Illinois ceremonies in honor and in memory of Abraham Lincoln were regularly a part of her life, and she early acquired much the same feeling for Lincoln that Edgar Lee Masters and Carl Sandburg and Vachel Lindsay were to experience. And of course it was Miss Monroe who during her editorship of *Poetry* magazine introduced such greater poets than herself as Lindsay and Sandburg to American readers.

She wrote two noteworthy poems on the subject of Lincoln. One makes up a section of her "Commemoration Ode," prepared for the World's Columbian Exposition in Chicago, October 21, 1892. Simply entitled "Lincoln," it is perhaps too excessive in its effects, and certainly not original in its conception of martyrdom, but it has enough merit to claim a place among the enduring tributes.

LINCOLN

And, lo! leading a blessed host comes one
 Who held a warring nation in his heart;
 Who knew love's agony, but had no part
In love's delight; whose mighty task was done
Through blood and tears that we might walk in joy,

85

And this day's rapture own no sad alloy.
Around him heirs of bliss, whose bright brows wear
Palm-leaves amid their laurels ever fair.
  Gaily they come, as though the drum
Beat out the call their glad hearts knew so well:
  Brothers once more, dear as of yore,
Who in a noble conflict nobly fell.
Their blood washed pure yon banner in the sky,
And quenched the brands laid 'neath these arches high—
The brave who, having fought, can never die.

Then surging through the vastness rise once more
The aureoled heirs of light, who onward bore
Through darksome times and trackless realms of ruth
The flag of beauty and the torch of truth.
They tore the mask from the foul face of wrong;
  Even to God's mysteries they dared aspire;
  High in the choir they built yon altar-fire,
And filled these aisles with color and with song:
The ever-young, the unfallen, wreathing for time
  Fresh garlands of the seeming-vanished years;
Faces long luminous, remote, sublime,
  And shining brows still dewy with our tears.
Back with the old glad smile comes one we knew—
  We bade him rear our house of joy today.
  But Beauty opened wide her starry way,
And he passed on. Bright champions of the true,
Soldiers of peace, seers, singers ever blest,—
From the wide ether of a loftier quest
Their winged souls throng our rites to glorify,—
The wise who, having known, can never die.

The other is a eulogy to Nancy Hanks, who had died in
October of 1818, when little Abe was only nine. The poem
is a lyrical lament for the mother "who gave us Lincoln and
never knew."

NANCY HANKS

Prairie child,
  Brief as dew,
What winds of wonder
  Nourished you?

Rolling plain
  Of billowy green,
Fair horizons,
  Blue, serene.

Lofty skies
  The slow clouds climb,
Where burning stars
  Beat out the time.

These, and the dreams
  Of fathers bold,
Baffled longings
  Hopes untold

Gave to you
  A heart of fire,
Love like waters,
  Brave desire.

Ah, when youth's rapture
  Went out in pain,
And all seemed over,
  Was all in vain?

O soul obscure,
  Whose wings life bound,
And soft death folded
  Under the ground.

Wilding lady,
   Still and true,
Who gave us Lincoln
   And never knew:

To you at last
   Our praise, our tears,
Love and a song
   Through the nation's years.

Mother of Lincoln,
   Our tears, our praise;
A battle-flag
   And the victor's bays!

Edgar Lee Masters

1869–1950

EDGAR LEE MASTERS, Vachel Lindsay, and Carl Sandburg are sometimes known as the Illinois poets. All spent their youth largely in the Land of Lincoln, and all three responded to the "Remember me!" of the ghost who walked the streets of Springfield. Two, Masters and Sandburg, have written more on Lincoln than almost any other American.

Masters tells us in his autobiography, *Across Spoon River*, how his interest in Lincoln grew. While he was still a boy (he was seventeen), the Masters family moved from their farm to Petersburg, which settlement Lincoln had surveyed in 1836, being at that time a deputy surveyor of Sangamon County and then residing at New Salem less than two miles up the Sangamon River from Petersburg.

In Petersburg stood the courthouse at which Lincoln came to try cases from 1843 until the time he was elected President. Masters' grandfather had in fact had Lincoln for a lawyer in a dispute over the purchase of a farm, a case which Lincoln lost. This is the courthouse Edgar Lee Masters knew as a boy and in which his father had his office as state's attorney.

The boy early acquired an interest in Lincoln, though regard had to suffer sometimes some qualification through judgments passed to him from his grandfather, whom Lincoln had disappointed. Actually, Masters never did hold

Lincoln in the esteem typical of most of the poets.

Masters tells us in *Across Spoon River* about his discovery that Lincoln's voice was high-keyed, having supposed it to be deep naturally. These impressions and others that he was to glean over the years were finally to take shape in a curious book, *Lincoln, the Man*, which Masters insisted was not strictly a biography, but rather "an examination of his mind and nature." It is a strange, virulent, vitriolic book, in fact the only completely unfavorable biography of Lincoln that has been published. Not surprisingly, it greatly offended Vachel Lindsay, but Masters attributed this to the wasting away of Lindsay's critical and historical faculties. Masters and Lindsay had been good friends throughout Lindsay's life, though they never saw each other after 1926, but it is possible *Lincoln, the Man* would have effected a breach in the relationship had not Lindsay committed suicide shortly after the book appeared.

Besides the biography, Masters wrote a great deal more on the subject of Abraham Lincoln, the Civil War, and its last catastrophe. He wrote a poetic drama in three acts on the assassination which is called *The Open Sea*. It accounts for the tragedy in terms suggested by the murder of Julius Caesar and sets out chiefly to narrate the life of Booth from infant to assassin through such lyrics as "A Man Child is Born," "John Wilkes Booth at the Farm," and "Junius Brutus Booth."

Masters also turned out a dramatic poem entitled *Lee* and a number of short lyrics inspired by the Civil War or the life of Lincoln, among them "Gettysburg" and "New Salem Hill," in *Invisible Landscapes*; "The Battle of Gettysburg," in *Poems of People*; and "The Lincoln and Douglas Debates," in *The Great Valley*.

But his finest achievement on the subject of Lincoln, though none is actually an elegy for the President, is to be found in three lyrics of the Spoon River volume: "Anne

Rutledge," "William H. Herndon," and "Hannah Arm-strong." These poems, together with "Fiddler Jones," are sometimes referred to as the New Salem group, and all are the imagined epitaphs of people close to Lincoln. Most familiar, and the best of the three, is "Anne Rutledge." Masters in his life of Lincoln did much to discredit the legend that suggests Lincoln felt a great romantic love for the girl, and it is a mistake to read the lyric as a product of that story. Instead it beautifully attributes to the influence of Anne's spirit the maturing of those qualities so conspicuous in Lincoln: charity, mercy, justice, and truth. Anne had been buried on her tragic death in August of 1835 in the old Concord cemetery near New Salem. But in 1890 her remains were removed to Oakland cemetery near Petersburg, and in 1921 there was erected at her new grave a monument on which is inscribed this poem.

ANNE RUTLEDGE

Out of me unworthy and unknown
The vibrations of deathless music;
"With malice toward none, with charity for all."
Out of me the forgiveness of millions toward millions,
And the beneficent face of a nation
Shining with justice and truth.
I am Anne Rutledge who sleep beneath these weeds,
Beloved in life of Abraham Lincoln,
Wedded to him, not through union,
But through separation.
Bloom forever, O Republic,
From the dust of my bosom!

"William H. Herndon" is the voice from the grave of Lincoln's law partner and friend. Herndon had also been a

friend and law partner of Masters' father. It had been
Herndon who had done most to solidify in the Lincoln lore
the Anne Rutledge legend. In his biography of Lincoln he
adduces to the fact of Lincoln's grief at the death of Anne
Rutledge an immense and continuing romantic love.
Earlier, in a lecture delivered at Springfield on November
16, 1866, he had declared that Lincoln had once remarked
that his heart was buried with Anne Rutledge. Herndon
and Lincoln's wife enjoyed little affection for each other
and his interpretation of the Anne Rutledge story did
nothing to improve their relationship.

Masters' poem is a direct tribute to Lincoln, imperishable
in the memory of a dying man.

WILLIAM H. HERNDON

There by the window in the old house
Perched on the bluff, overlooking miles of valley,
My days of labor closed, sitting out life's decline,
Day by day did I look in my memory,
As one who gazes in an enchantress' crystal globe,
And I saw the figures of the past,
As if in a pageant glassed by a shining dream,
Move through the incredible sphere of time.
And I saw a man arise from the soil like a fabled giant
And throw himself over a deathless destiny,
Master of great armies, head of the republic,
Bringing together into a dithyramb of recreative song
The epic hopes of a people;
At the same time Vulcan of sovereign fires,
Where imperishable shields and swords were beaten out
From spirits tempered in heaven.
Look in the crystal! See how he hastens on
To the place where his path comes up to the path

Of a child of *Plutarch* and *Shakespeare*.
O Lincoln, actor indeed, playing well your part,
And Booth, who strode in a mimic play within the play,
Often and often I saw you,
As the cawing crows winged their way to the wood
Over my house-top at solemn sunsets,
There by my window,
Alone.

Hannah Armstrong kept the inn at New Salem in which Lincoln lived. She was the mother of Duff Armstrong, whom Lincoln successfully defended against the charge of murder in the widely celebrated "almanac" trial. Some readers believe that the subject-speaker of Spoon River's "Fiddler Jones" is Hannah Armstrong's brother; some believe it is her son John, who had been an acquaintance of the poet's father in Petersburg. John Armstrong, like William Herndon, is buried in Oak Ridge Cemetery, Springfield, close to the tomb of Abraham Lincoln. Hannah Armstrong's epitaph points to the thing which most distinguished her life—her friendship with Abraham Lincoln.

HANNAH ARMSTRONG

I wrote him a letter asking him for old times' sake
To discharge my sick boy from the army;
But maybe he couldn't read it.
Then I went to town and had James Garber,
Who wrote beautifully, write him a letter;
But maybe that was lost in the mails.
So I traveled all the way to Washington.
I was more than an hour finding the White House.
And when I found it they turned me away,
Hiding their smiles. Then I thought:

"Oh, well, he ain't the same as when I boarded him
And he and my husband worked together
And all of us called him Abe, there in Menard."
As a last attempt I turned to a guard and said:
"Please say it's old Aunt Hannah Armstrong
From Illinois, come to see him about her sick boy
In the army."
Well, just in a moment they let me in!
And when he saw me he broke in a laugh,
And dropped his business as president,
And wrote in his own hand Doug's discharge,
Talking the while of the early days,
And telling stories.

Carl Sandburg

1878–

THE only one of the Illinois group of poets yet living, Carl Sandburg like the others came by his enthusiasm for Lincoln early and naturally. But more so than any of the others, perhaps more so than any other single person, Sandburg has dedicated his life to the perpetuation of the Lincoln saga. For his monumental biography, *The Prairie Years*, published in 1926, and *The War Years*, published in 1939, the poet has for a long time now been acknowledged the leading authority on Lincoln lore. Over the years he has assembled the testimony of the historical records and the anecdotes familiar to those who knew Long Abraham to put together an impressive study of the man and the President.

He has produced a very library of Lincoln works. He collaborated with Paul Angle to write a biography of the controversial Mary Todd, *Mary Lincoln, Wife and Widow*; he has composed a *Preface to Lincoln*; he has produced a Lincoln reader and a Lincoln miscellany. On February 12, 1959, he spoke before Congress on Abraham Lincoln. And on March 9, 1961, upon the occasion of Lincoln's one hundredth inaugural anniversary, he delivered an address at the east front of the U. S. Capitol. And he has done a great deal more besides, in his writing and in public appearances, to account for the life and times of Abraham Lincoln.

One would expect then to find the poetry of Sandburg

alive with his impressions of Lincoln. And so it is. In a whole host of free verse lyrics, in such serenely beautiful poems as "Cool Tombs" and "Grass," for example, occur references to the assassination and to Gettysburg. And perhaps a score of poems have as their primary subject the figure of the President. But Sandburg's two most impressive verse portraits are to be found in a long passage in *The People, Yes* and the poem "The Long Shadow of Lincoln."

The first is a study of Lincoln as a "mystery in smoke and flags." Much of the poetry is by Lincoln himself, for Sandburg quotes him liberally, thereby proving him one of our best poets. Lincoln, declares the poet, "spoke one verse for then and now." This, as we have seen, is a recurring theme among the poets.

from
THE PEOPLE, YES

Lincoln?
He was a mystery in smoke and flags
saying yes to the smoke, yes to the flags,
yes to the paradoxes of democracy,
yes to the hopes of government
of the people by the people for the people,
no to debauchery of the public mind,
no to personal malice nursed and fed,
yes to the Constitution when a help,
no to the Constitution when a hindrance,
yes to man as a struggler amid illusions,
each man fated to answer for himself:
Which of the faiths and illusions of mankind
must I choose for my own sustaining light
to bring me beyond the present wilderness?

Lincoln? was he a poet?
and did he write verses?
"I have not willingly planted a thorn in any man's
bosom."
"I shall do nothing through malice; what I deal with
is too vast for malice."

Death was in the air.
So was birth.
What was dying few could say.
What was being born none could know.

He took the wheel in a lashing roaring hurricane.
And by what compass did he steer the course of
the ship?
"My policy is to have no policy," he said in the
early months,
And three years later, "I have been controlled by
events."

He could play with the wayward human mind, saying at
Charleston, Illinois, September 18, 1858, it was no
answer to an argument to call a man a liar.
"I assert that you [pointing a finger in the face of a man in
the crowd] are here today, and you undertake to prove
me a liar by showing that you were in Mattoon yesterday.
"I say that you took your hat off your head and you prove
me a liar by putting it on your head."

He saw personal liberty across wide horizons.
"Our progress in degeneracy appears to me to be pretty
rapid," he wrote Joshua F. Speed, August 24, 1855.

"As a nation we began by declaring that 'all men are
created equal, except negroes.' When the Know-Noth-
ings get control, it will read 'all men are created equal

except negroes and foreigners and Catholics.' When it
comes to this, I shall prefer emigrating to some country
where they make no pretense of loving liberty."

> Did he look deep into a crazy pool
> and see the strife and wrangling
> with a clear eye, writing the military
> head of a stormswept area:
> "If both factions, or neither, shall abuse
> you, you will probably be about right. Be-
> ware of being assailed by one and praised
> by the other"?

> Lincoln? was he a historian?
> did he know mass chaos?
> did he have an answer for those
> who asked him to organize chaos?

"Actual war coming, blood grows hot, and blood is spilled.
Thought is forced from old channels into confusion.
Deception breeds and thrives. Confidence dies and
universal suspicion reigns.

"Each man feels an impulse to kill his neighbor, lest he
be first killed by him. Revenge and retaliation follow.
And all this, as before said, may be among honest
men only; but this is not all.

"Every foul bird comes abroad and every dirty reptile rises
up. These add crime to confusion.

"Strong measures, deemed indispensable, but harsh at best,
such men make worse by mal administration. Murders
for old grudges, and murders for pelf, proceed under
any cloak that will best cover for the occasion. These
causes amply account for what has happened in Missouri."

Early in '64 the Committee of the New York Working-
man's Democratic Republican Association called on

him with assurances and he meditated aloud for them,
recalling race and draft riots:

"The most notable feature of a disturbance in your
    city last summer was the hanging of some working
    people by other working people. It should never
    be so.

"The strongest bond of human sympathy, outside of
    the family relation, should be one uniting all
    working people, of all nations and tongues and
    kindreds.

"Let not him who is houseless pull down the house
    of another, but let him labor diligently and build
    one for himself, thus by example assuring that his
    own shall be safe from violence when built."

Lincoln? did he gather
the feel of the American dream
and see its kindred over the earth?

"As labor is the common burden of our race,
so the effort of some to shift
their share of the burden
onto the shoulders of others
is the great durable curse of the race."

    "I hold,
if the Almighty had ever made a set of men
that should do all of the eating
and none of the work,
he would have made them
with mouths only, and no hands;
and if he had ever made another class,
that he had intended should do all the work
and none of the eating,
he would have made them
without mouths and all hands."

"—the same spirit that says, 'You toil and work and earn bread, and I'll eat it.' No matter in what shape it comes, whether from the mouth of a king who seeks to bestride the people of his own nation and live by the fruit of their labor, or from one race of men as an apology for enslaving another race, it is the same tyrannical principle."

"As I would not be a slave, so I would not be a master. This expresses my idea of democracy. Whatever differs from this, to the extent of the difference, is no democracy."

"I never knew a man who wished to be himself a slave. Consider if you know any good thing that no man desires for himself."

"The sheep and the wolf
   are not agreed upon a definition
   of the word liberty."

"The whole people of this nation
   will ever do well
   if well done by."

"The plainest print cannot be read
   through a gold eagle."

"How does it feel to be President?" an Illinois friend asked.
"Well, I'm like the man they rode out of town on a rail. He said if it wasn't for the honor of it he would just as soon walk."

> Lincoln? he was a dreamer.
> He saw the ships at sea,
> he saw himself living and dead
> in dreams that came.

Into a secretary's diary December 23, 1863 went an entry: "The President tonight had a dream. He was in a party of plain people, and as it became known who he was, they began to comment on his appearance. One of them said: 'He is a very common-looking man.' The President replied: 'The Lord prefers common-looking people. That is the reason he makes so many of them.' "

He spoke one verse for then and now:
> "If we could first know where we are,
> and whither we are tending,
> we could better judge
> what to do, and how to do it."

"The Long Shadow of Lincoln" was read as the Phi Beta Kappa poem at the College of William and Mary in December of 1944, during the dark hours of the Second World War. In this poem, as in Lindsay's "Abraham Lincoln Walks at Midnight," Lincoln's shadow stands for Peace and "the hard old teaching: 'We must disenthrall ourselves.' " The poetry here is the poetry of Whitman's "Lilacs" and *The Gettysburg Address*.

THE LONG SHADOW OF LINCOLN

(A Litany)

We can succeed only by concert. . . . The dogmas of the quiet past are inadequate to the stormy present. The occasion is piled high with difficulty, and we must rise with the occasion. As our case is new, so we must think anew and act anew. We must disenthrall ourselves . . . *December 1, 1862. The President's Message to Congress.*

> Be sad, be cool, be kind,
> Remembering those now dream-dust

Hallowed in the ruts and gullies,
Solemn bones under the smooth blue sea,
Faces war-blown in a falling rain.

Be a brother, if so can be,
To those beyond battle fatigue
Each in his own corner of earth
Or forty fathoms undersea
Beyond all boom of guns,
Beyond any bong of a great bell,
Each with a bosom and number,
Each with a pack of secrets,
Each with a personal dream and doorway,
And over them now the long endless winds
With the low healing song of time,
The hush and sleep murmur of time.
Make your wit a guard and cover.
Sing low, sing high, sing wide.
Let your laughter come free
Remembering looking toward peace:
"We must disenthrall ourselves."

Be a brother, if so can be,
To those thrown forward
For taking hard-won lines,
For holding hard-won points
And their reward so-so.
Little they care to talk about,
Their pay held in a mute calm,
High-spot memories going unspoken;
What they did being past words,
What they took being hard won.
Be sad, be kind, be cool.
Weep if you must,
And weep, open and shameless,
Before these altars.

There are wounds past words.
There are cripples less broken
Than many who walk whole.
There are dead youths
With wrists of silence
Who keep a vast music
Under their shut lips;
What they did being past words;
Their dreams, like their deaths,
Beyond any smooth and easy telling;
Having given till no more to give.

There is dust alive
With dreams of the Republic,
With dreams of the family of man
Flung wide on a shrinking globe;
With old timetables,
Old maps, old guideposts
Torn into shreds,
Shot into tatters,
Burnt in a fire wind,
Lost in the shambles,
Faded in rubble and ashes.

There is dust alive.
Out of a granite tomb,
Out of a bronze sarcophagus,
Loose from the stone and copper
Steps a white-smoke ghost,
Lifting an authoritative hand
In the name of dreams worth dying for,
In the name of men whose dust breathes
Of those dreams so worth dying for;
What they did being past words,
Beyond all smooth and easy telling.

Be sad, be kind, be cool,
Remembering, under God, a dream-dust
Hallowed in the ruts and gullies,
Solemn bones under the smooth blue sea,
Faces war-blown in a falling rain.

Sing low, sing high, sing wide.
Make your wit a guard and cover.
Let your laughter come free,
Like a help and a brace of comfort.

The earth laughs, the sun laughs
Over every wise harvest of man,
Over man looking toward peace
By the light of the hard old teaching:
"We must disenthrall ourselves."

Vachel Lindsay
1879–1931

THE home that Vachel Lindsay knew as a boy in
Springfield, Illinois, was just a little piece away from
the old Lincoln home, which from the time of Lindsay's
birth was a museum. And, if the legend can be depended
upon, Lincoln had slept in the very room in which Lindsay
was born.

Edgar Lee Masters in his life of Lindsay tells us of the
poet's early association with Lincoln:

The custodian of the Lincoln home liked children and he
allowed Vachel . . . to play in the historic rooms and to look at
the cartoons and pictures which covered the walls, depicting
events North and South before the War. On these occasions
G. A. R. veterans frequently would be passing from picture to
picture, talking over the events of the War, and what Lincoln
and his generals had done, or had failed to do, and of the
successes and misadventures of famous battles. The poet was
eight or nine years old when he was listening to such things; so
that he grew up on Lincoln.

Like Masters himself, Lindsay, though, experienced con-
flicting emotions concerning Lincoln. The influence of the
boy's family was not unfelt, and his father, a staunch
Democrat who had removed to Illinois from Kentucky, was
constantly reminding the lad that the President had no
right to free the slaves of the South, to rob and to make
destitute so many Southern families.

But Lindsay eventually resolved such difficulties, and

105

came round to a Whitman-like idolatry of Abraham Lincoln. He was to write often and with passion in praise of the "master of us all." In "Adventures While Singing these Songs," an autobiographical preface to his *Collected Poems*, he remarked:

Those who hate the George Gray Barnard statue of Abraham Lincoln seem to think their hero has always been a steel engraving of a man in a Prince Albert coat and decorously trimmed whiskers. They have seen this so often on the back of the dollar bill that they believe it. But Ruby [his cousin and playmate] and I knew better than that about Lincoln. He was a profound volcano, producing, incidentally, ferocious debate.

Lindsay is today buried in his native Springfield, not very far from the man to whom he was so devoted.

But before his tragic suicide in 1931, Lindsay had produced within the wealth of poetry that was his a number of poetic tributes to Lincoln. One of these was distributed as a little pamphlet in 1909 at the time Springfield was observing the centenary of Lincoln's birth. Described in its first title as "A Memorial to Lincoln Called The Horses of Time," it became after some revision the "Litany of the Heroes." It is a poem illustrating the position of Abraham Lincoln among the dominating personalities of history. After a prologue, the poet pays his respects to twenty-one immortals of the past, among them Caesar, Socrates, Christ, Shakespeare, Milton, and Napoleon. The last tribute is to Abraham Lincoln and could have been written only by the Springfield poet. Lincoln he finds representative of the American spirit in history.

from
LITANY OF THE HEROES

Would I might rouse the Lincoln in you all,
That which is gendered in the wilderness

From lonely prairies and God's tenderness,
Imperial soul, star of a weedy stream,
Born where the ghosts of buffaloes still dream,
Whose spirit hoof-beats storm above his grave—
Above that breast of earth and prairie-fire—
Fire that freed the slave.

In the poem "Babylon, Babylon, Babylon the Great" Lindsay's subject is the Lincoln of Cooper Union, whom we already know something about through William Cullen Bryant. According to the poem, and the poet's accompanying notes, Lincoln at Cooper Union had thrown away his prepared speech and continued to speak from inspiration. This does not seem to be in accord with the facts as we know them. We do know that Lincoln rejected the corrections he had solicited from Joseph Medill and Charles Ray, who were publisher and editor-in-chief of the *Chicago Tribune*. And we do know that he thoroughly revised the text when he learned the speech was to be delivered in Manhattan rather than in Brooklyn. But this was two days before that memorable Monday evening and not in the course of the evening itself.

Many vivid impressions of Lincoln that evening have survived, all noting his singular dress and manner, and all flattering to his effect on the assembly. Typical is the recollection of Joseph H. Choate, later President McKinley's Ambassador to Great Britain but present that night as a young man of twenty-eight: "At first sight there was nothing impressive or imposing about him; his clothes hung awkwardly on his giant frame; his face was of a dark pallor without the slightest tinge of colour; his seamed and rugged features bore the furrows of hardship and struggle; his deep-set eyes looked sad and anxious; his countenance in repose gave little evidence of the brilliant power which raised him from the lowest to the highest station among his countrymen; as he talked to me before the meeting he seemed ill at ease. . . . When he spoke, he was transformed; his eyes kindled, his voice rang, his face shone and seemed to light up the whole assembly. For an hour and a half he held the audience in the hollow of his hand." [10]

About Lincoln's electric effect on the audience that night there can be no question. Indeed, most historians are agreed that the Cooper Union speech is the single event which did most to catapult Lincoln into the nomination. But Lindsay in his poem is celebrating the genius for invention or improvisation. In a note to the lyric he declared that he was exhorting Sandburg to improvise, "but in a way the opposite of jazz—for I have always hated jazz, as our most Babylonian disease." He calls upon his fellow Illinois poet to march with simple and mighty Lincoln, "that tall prophet," against Babylon. And this, of course, Carl Sandburg has long been most happy to do.

The poem first appeared in *The New York Evening Post*, in Christopher Morley's Bowling Green column, as a tribute to Carl Sandburg on the occasion of a visit by the poet to New York. Lindsay has reported that he had the poem printed several months later in Memphis, Tennessee, "in anticipation of Carl Sandburg's visit to address Memphis in a recital for the Goodwyn Institute, November 17, 1923." It was issued, he tells us, "in a three-foot broadside, with my picture of Babylon at the top as a kind of hieroglyphic."

BABYLON, BABYLON, BABYLON THE GREAT

(Inscribed to Carl Sandburg)

This poem is based on the episode of "Lincoln's Lost Speech," too dangerous to print at the time, at Cooper Union, his first appearance in the East.

[10] Quoted in Lord Godfrey Rathbone Benson Charnwood, *Abraham Lincoln* (Garden City, N. Y.: Garden City Publishing Co., 1929), p. 155.

Isaiah, the country-boy, marched against the jazz—
Babylon the shrewd and slick, Babylon the great.
Jeremiah, Ezekiel, Daniel, walked alone,
Alone against Babylon, alone against fate.
St. Paul walked alone, St. Peter walked alone,
Against that town to marvel on, Babylon the great.

Lincoln at Cooper Union, improvised and chanted,
Threw away his speech, and told tales out of school,
Changed from politician to God's divine fool.
Beside himself, beyond himself, set his old heart free,
The flame spread, the flame spread, every suppressed word
    was said,
Isaiah's voice from the dead;
Lincoln's great lost speech, nowhere written down,
But it burned every gate of the famous old town.

Lincoln at Cooper Union, called down fire from Heaven,
Overthrew jazz—Babylon, Babylon the great.

I have seen the burning of Babylon's gardens,
Many and many a noble day.
I have watched the ashes of that beautiful lost city,
Blown through many a year away.

Statesmen have torn down Babylon. . . . The gophers
    have buried Babylon. . . .
Coyotes lope through Babylon. . . . Prairie dogs bore the
    clay and sand. . . .
Texas cattle have trampled Babylon deeper in dung and
    dust. . . .
But forever stands Babylon, fresh in the sunrise, . . .
Foam upon the ocean . . . or granite on the land,
As new as the Devil, and the Devil's lust.

How our tales of Babylon multiply upon the ranges!
How old memories of victory renew!
Except for the warfare of the youngsters against Babylon,
The campfire songs would be few.

Troubador!—March with bleeding feet against Babylon!—
(So, keep going to the sun! So, keep going to the sun!)
—If you would be a man.—As these have done before!
As lonely as Lincoln, dazed in Babylon,
Plod, plod, with a heartache, through the Devil's own
    door!
Tear up your set speeches, improvise once more!

War must begin against that city's music,
So—sing a silly song. Say:—"The sky is blue."
Sing a song of rainbow gems, unknown to Babylon.
Then improvise a song of the mick who lifts the hod,
Of the mick who sets in concrete the steel truss and rod,
Who builds the auto highways across the prairie sod—
(So, keep going to the sun! So, keep going to the sun!)
Improvise a cowboy song, of cactus and of dew,
And of raging on a mustang across the alkali
To where the snow-bright mountains of new mediation lie,
To the Indian basket-flowers, the ferns, the meadow-rue;—
Sing of beans in the pod, and of wheat in the shock,
Of hay in the stack, and windmills in the air,
Of castellated silos, and turkeys fat and fair,
Of chickens and of guineas, of pheasants, quails and eagles,
Of the High-School senior boys, foot-ball players, Sheiks
    and swells,
Of Lincoln-highway roses and sweet lovers everywhere:—
And the candies and the vanities of senior High-School
    belles,
(So, keep going to the sun! So, keep going to the sun!)

Sing a Kansas love-song, modest, clean and true.
Sing a Kansas love-song, modest, clean and true.
Then lift your psalm of the Manna of our God!
It is the only way to go into Babylon,
Call down fire from Heaven, and the world renew.

This is the only way a bard is a man.
So lift your proud word against the towers if you can.
Go on, with your guitar, through the Devil's breezy gate.
March on, with simple Lincoln against Babylon, Babylon,—
His dog-eared carpet-bag crammed with state papers,
His sweaty old duster flapping like a rag.—
Go, with prairie Lincoln against Babylon, Babylon,
Go with that tall prophet, again to Cooper Union,
March with mighty Lincoln against Babylon the Great!
(So—keep going to the sun! So—keep going to the sun!)

In another poem, a short, light lyric, Lindsay describes Lincoln's arrival in Springfield. And clearly that little Illinois town, as the prairie-lawyer is himself made to recognize, is a significant stepping stone.

WHEN LINCOLN CAME TO SPRINGFIELD

When Lincoln came to Springfield,
    In the ancient days,
Queer were the streets and sketchy,
    And he was in a maze.

Leaving log cabins behind him
    For the mud streets of this place,
Sorrow for Anne Rutledge
    Burned in his face.

He threw his muddy saddle bags
    On Joshua Speed's floor,
He took off his old hat,
    He looked around the store.

He shook his long hair
    On his bison-head,
He sat down on the counter,
    "Speed, I've moved," he said.

By way of paying homage to Nancy Hanks, mother of Lincoln, Lindsay in another poem acknowledges the role played by mothers in the history of heroes. He refers us to the mother of Buffalo Bill, to the mother of Barnum, to the mother of Mark Twain, and to Theodore Roosevelt's heritage, in order to lead climactically to a girl "who slept in dust and sorrow." With its flippant rhymes the poem is almost playful until it arrives at the last three lines.

NANCY HANKS, MOTHER OF ABRAHAM LINCOLN

"Out of the eater came forth meat; and out of the strong
    came forth sweetness." Judges 14:14

    A sweet girl graduate, lean as a fawn,
    The very whimsy of time,
    Read her class upon Commencement Day—
    A trembling filigree rhyme.
    The pansy that blooms on the window sill,
    Blooms in exactly the proper place;
    And she nodded just like a pansy there,
    And her poem was all about bowers and showers,
    Sugary streamlet and mossy rill,
    All about daisies on dale and hill—
    And she was the mother of Buffalo Bill.

    Another girl, a cloud-drift sort,
    Dreamlit, moonlit, marble-white,
    Light-footed saint on the pilgrim shore,
    The best since New England fairies began,
    Was the mother of Barnum, the circus man.

    A girl from Missouri, snippy and vain,
    As frothy a miss as any you know,
    A wren, a toy, a pink silk bow,

The belle of the choir, she drove insane
Missouri deacons and all the sleek,
Her utter tomfoolery made men weak,
Till they could not stand and they could not speak.
Oh, queen of fifteen and sixteen,
Missouri sweetened beneath her reign—
And she was the mother of bad Mark Twain.

Not always are lions born of lions,
Roosevelt sprang from a palace of lace;
On the other hand is the dizzy truth:
Not always is beauty born of beauty.
Some treasures wait in a hidden place.
All over the world were thousands of belles.
In far-off eighteen hundred and nine,
Girls of fifteen, girls of twenty,
Their mammas dressed them up a-plenty—
Each garter was bright, each stocking fine,
But for all their innocent devices,
Their cheeks of fruit and their eyes of wine,
And each voluptuous design,
And all soft glories that we trace
In Europe's palaces of lace,
A girl who slept in dust and sorrow,
Nancy Hanks, in a lost cabin,
Nancy Hanks had the loveliest face!

But Lindsay's most beautiful poetic tribute to Lincoln, some would say the finest lyric he ever composed, is the famous "Abraham Lincoln Walks at Midnight." Written at the time of the First World War, and one of the most familiar poems of that day, the lyric presents the spirit of the prairie-lawyer restlessly pacing the streets of Springfield, unable to sleep upon his hill again until peace is insured for all peoples across the world. In the poet's vision Lincoln at midnight passes up and down before the old courthouse which had been the scene of his many trials. He lives again, once more assumes the cares of state and the woes of the world. He will always be among us. He cannot die, he cannot rest, until all people are brothers.

Magnificent in conception, the poem is most impressive for its lyrical effects, for the way in which is captured the slow but restless pacing of the perturbed spirit.

ABRAHAM LINCOLN WALKS AT MIDNIGHT

It is portentous, and a thing of state
That here at midnight, in our little town
A mourning figure walks, and will not rest,
Near the old court-house pacing up and down,

Or by his homestead, or in shadowed yards
He lingers where his children used to play,
Or through the market, on the well-worn stones
He stalks until the dawn-stars burn away.

A bronzed, lank man! His suit of ancient black,
A famous high-top hat and plain worn shawl
Make him the quaint great figure that men love,
The prairie-lawyer, master of us all.

He cannot sleep upon his hillside now.
He is among us:—as in times before!
And we who toss and lie awake for long,
Breathe deep, and start, to see him pass the door.

His head is bowed. He thinks of men and kings.
Yea, when the sick world cries, how can he sleep?
Too many peasants fight, they know not why;
Too many homesteads in black terror weep.

The sins of all the war-lords burn his heart.
He sees the dreadnaughts scouring every main.
He carries on his shawl-wrapped shoulders now
The bitterness, the folly and the pain.

He cannot rest until a spirit-dawn
Shall come;—the shining hope of Europe free:
A league of sober folk, the workers' earth,
Bringing long peace to Cornland, Alp and Sea.

It breaks his heart that kings must murder still,
That all his hours of travail here for men
Seem yet in vain. And who will bring white peace
That he may sleep upon his hill again?

John Gould Fletcher

1886–1950

WHILE Vachel Lindsay and Masters and Sandburg were reared in an atmosphere that radiated Lincoln, John Gould Fletcher grew up in the Deep South. Like Lindsay, though, Fletcher was moved by the horror of the First World War to reflect on the gaunt figure standing in the ashes of the War Between the States. He tells us in his autobiography, *Life is My Song,* how during the last weeks in March and the first two weeks of April 1916 he had been reading several books on the Civil War, having determined to "investigate the life and character of Abraham Lincoln," who had never been "real" to him. He pored over William H. Herndon's "homespun, but honest, biography," and through it was led to see Lincoln "in a new light, as the last of the heroic pioneers who had conquered this continent between the Louisiana Purchase of 1803 and the discovery of gold in California in 1849."

The result of all this was a beautiful and immensely popular poem. Fletcher himself accounts for its inception:

On April 19, 1916, the day of the anniversary of the battle of Lexington, I sat down to write my poem on Abraham Lincoln —the first truly patriotic poem I had written, patriotic in the same sense that Emerson's "Concord Hymn" and Whitman's "Drum-Taps" and Moody's "Ode in the Time of Hesitation" had all been patriotic poems. It was also the first poem I had written in which my mind came to terms with the Anglo-Saxon strength of Biblical phraseology; the first I had written in which I said plainly that the epoch of America's pioneer strength and greatness lay in the past, not in the present; the first I had written in which the technique of imagism was complemented by stanzas expressive of nothing but plain, unabashed, didactic purpose.

His "Lincoln" was the first poem since his return to America in the fall of 1914 which did not have as its first reader Amy Lowell. Fletcher placed the poem, without her help, in a new poetry magazine appearing in Boston and was paid for it, as he recalls, $15.00—"a miserable sum compared with what I knew to be its worth. . . ."

But readers were at once enthusiastic about the ode and doubtless the piece had something to do with Fletcher's winning the Pulitzer Award in 1939 for his *Selected Poems*.

In London after the armistice Sara Teasdale's husband brought him the news that "the writing of a single poem, my 'Lincoln,' had made me one of the most discussed poets of the day, after my departure, someone to be mentioned in the same breath with Vachel Lindsay and Amy Lowell. Since 'Lincoln' had been a poem written to fit a special occasion—the occasion being America's entry in the War, which this poem anticipated by a full year—I did not suppose my work would continue to have the popularity this particular work had given it."

Indeed the poem, which like Lindsay's "Abraham Lincoln Walks at Midnight" identifies Lincoln with the pioneer spirit, deserves the praise it had initially and continues to receive. Its free verse is very unlike that of Walt Whitman or Carl Sandburg but is yet beautifully lyrical. Not the least of its virtues is the magnificent opening metaphor, which recalls the closing lines of Markham's poem.

LINCOLN

I

Like a gaunt, scraggly pine
Which lifts its head above the mournful sandhills;
And patiently, through dull years of bitter silence,
Untended and uncared for, begins to grow.

Ungainly, laboring, huge,
The wind of the north has twisted and gnarled its
  branches;
Yet in the heat of midsummer days, when thunder-clouds
  ring the horizon,
A nation of men shall rest beneath its shade.

And it shall protect them all,
Hold everyone safe there, watching aloof in silence;
Until at last one mad stray bolt from the zenith
Shall strike it in an instant down to earth.

II

There was a darkness in this man; an immense and hollow
  darkness,
Of which we may not speak, nor share with him, nor enter;
A darkness through which strong roots stretched down-
  wards into the earth
Towards old things;
Towards the herdman-kings who walked the earth and
  spoke with God,
Towards the wanderers who sought for they knew not
  what, and found their goal at last;
Towards the men who waited, only waited patiently when
  all seemed lost,
Many bitter winters of defeat;
Down to the granite of patience

These roots swept, knotted fibrous roots, prying, piercing,
 seeking,
And drew from the living rock and the living waters about
 it
The red sap to carry upwards to the sun.

Not proud, but humble,
Only to serve and pass on, to endure to the end through
 service;
For the ax is laid at the root of the trees, and all that bring
 not forth good fruit
Shall be cut down on the day to come and cast into the
 fire.

III

There is silence abroad in the land today,
And in the hearts of men, a deep and anxious silence;
And, because we are still at last, those bronze lips slowly
 open,
Those hollow and weary eyes take on a gleam of light.

Slowly a patient, firm-syllabled voice cuts through the end-
 less silence
Like laboring oxen that drag a plow through the chaos of
 rude clay-fields:
"I went forward as the light goes forward in early spring,
But there were also many things which I left behind.

"Tombs that were quiet;
One, of a mother, whose brief light went out in the
 darkness,
One, of a loved one, the snow on whose grave is long-
 falling,
One, only of a child, but it was mine.

"Have you forgot your graves? Go, question them in
 anguish,

Listen long to their unstirred lips. From your hostages to
    silence,
Learn there is no life without death, no dawn without sun-
    setting,
No victory but to Him who has given all."

IV

The clamor of cannon dies down, the furnace-mouth of
    the battle is silent.
The midwinter sun dips and descends, the earth takes on
    afresh its bright colors.
But he whom we mocked and obeyed not, he whom we
    scorned and mistrusted,
He has descended, like a god, to his rest.

Over the uproar of cities,
Over the million intricate threads of life wavering and
    crossing,
In the midst of problems we know not, tangling, per-
    plexing, ensnaring,
Rises one white tomb alone.
Beam over it, stars.
Wrap it round, stripes—stripes red for the pain that he
    bore for you—
Enfold it forever, O flag, rent, soiled, but repaired through
    your anguish;
Long as you keep him there safe, the nations shall bow
    to your law.

Strew over him flowers:
Blue forget-me-nots from the north, and the bright pink
    arbutus
From the east, and from the west rich orange blossoms,
But from the heart of the land take the passion-flower;

Rayed, violet, dim,
With the nails that pierced, the cross that he bore and the
  circlet,
And beside it there lay also one lonely snow-white mag-
  nolia,
Bitter for remembrance of the healing which has passed.

James Oppenheim

1882–1932

M INNESOTA-born James Oppenheim identifies Lincoln with love of country, with a sense of brotherhood, with freedom, and with peace. Intensely pacifist, as editor of *The Seven Arts* magazine he vigorously and courageously opposed the entry of America into the First World War. And like so many others, notably Vachel Lindsay and John Gould Fletcher, he called upon the spirit of Lincoln to "guard our land at midnight."

Oppenheim had earlier published in *Monday Morning and Other Poems* (1909) a long poem on Lincoln, an account of his growth from prairie child to President. It is not a great poem and Oppenheim himself did not cherish it, but it does include some inspired lines. For the poet Lincoln is "Our huge Atlantic coast-storm in a shawl" and "Our cyclone in a smile." Like Lindsay, he too would rouse the Lincoln in us all, which means exciting the passions of love and brotherhood. And then would America become:

> . . . a vast World-Torch
> Flaming a faith across the dying Earth,
> Proclaiming from the Atlantic's rocky porch,
> That a New World was struggling at the Birth!

Unhappily Oppenheim's ardor for social justice, his passionate dedication to the democratic principles, and his deep spiritual and moral convictions found their voice in no deep well of poetry. In over-Whitmanated song, the didactic all too conspicuous, he produced a great many mortal poems. But when for his themes he abandoned politics he achieved sometimes exciting lyrical heights.

One such instance occurs in another poem on the subject of Lincoln. This is the haunting "Memories of Whitman and Lincoln," which was published in 1924 in *The Sea*, a collection of Oppenheim's best poems. Written in the loose free-verse style of Whitman himself, the lyric is a hymn to the spring that throbs through America and that is kept vital and alive by the memory of Two Brothers.

The poet here acknowledges that in the kindred spirits of Walt Whitman and Abraham Lincoln are best expressed and made manifest the ideals of the young country. At the same time, through its epigraph and its lilacs theme the lyric suggests that perhaps the finest elegy for Lincoln and the supreme tribute to the memory of the President remains Whitman's mighty symphony of sound and symbol.

MEMORIES OF WHITMAN AND LINCOLN

"When lilacs last in the dooryard bloom'd"
—W. W.

Lilacs shall bloom for Walt Whitman
And lilacs for Abraham Lincoln.
Spring hangs in the dew of the dooryards
These memories—these memories—
They hang in the dew for the bard who fetched
A sprig of them once for his brother
When he lay cold and dead . . .
And forever now when America leans in the dooryard
And over the hills Spring dances,
Smell of lilacs and sight of lilacs shall bring to her heart
these brothers . . .

Lilacs shall bloom for Walt Whitman
And lilacs for Abraham Lincoln.

Who are the shadow-forms crowding the night?
What shadows of men?
The stilled star-night is high with these brooding spirits—
Their shoulders rise on the Earth-rim, and they are great
  presences in heaven—
They move through the stars like outlined winds in young-
  leaved maples.

Lilacs bloom for Walt Whitman
And lilacs for Abraham Lincoln.

Deeply the nation throbs with a world's anguish—
But it sleeps, and I on the housetops
Commune with souls long dead who guard our land at
  midnight,
A strength in each hushed heart—
I seem to hear the Atlantic moaning on our shores with
  the plaint of the dying
And rolling on our shores with the rumble of battle . . .
I seem to see my country growing golden toward
  California,
And, as fields of daisies, a people, with slumbering up-
  turned faces
Leaned over by Two Brothers,
And the greatness that is gone.

Lilacs bloom for Walt Whitman
And lilacs for Abraham Lincoln.

Spring runs over the land,
A young girl, light-footed, eager . . .
For I hear a song that is faint and sweet with first love,
Out of the West, fresh with the grass and the timber,
But dreamily soothing the sleepers . . .
I listen: I drink it deep . . .

Softly the Spring sings,
Softly and clearly:

"I open lilacs for the beloved,
Lilacs for the lost, the dead.
And, see, for the living, I bring
      sweet strawberry blossoms,
And I bring buttercups, and I bring to
      the woods anemones and bluebells . . .
I open lilacs for the beloved,
And when my fluttering garment drifts through
      dusty cities,
And blows on hills, and brushes the inland sea,
Over you, sleepers, over you, tired sleepers,
A fragrant memory falls . . .
I open love in the shut heart,
I open lilacs for the beloved."

Lilacs bloom for Walt Whitman
And lilacs for Abraham Lincoln.

Was that the Spring that sang, opening locked hearts,
And is remembrance mine?
For I know these two great shadows in the spacious night,
Shadows folding America close between them,
Close to the heart . . .
And I know how my own lost youth grew up blessedly
   in their spirit,
And how the morning song of the mighty native bard
Sent me out from my dreams to the living America,
To the chanting seas, to the piney hills, down the railroad
   vistas,
Out into the streets of Manhattan when the whistles blew
   at seven,
Down to the mills of Pittsburgh and the rude faces of
   labor . . .

And I know how the grave great music of that other,
Music in which lost armies sang requiems,
And the vision of that gaunt, that great and solemn figure,
And the graven face, the deep eyes, the mouth,
O human-hearted brother,
Dedicated anew my undevoted heart
To America, my land.

Lilacs bloom for Walt Whitman
And lilacs for Abraham Lincoln.

Now in this hour I was suppliant to these two brothers,
And I said: Your land has need:
Half-awakened and blindly we grope in the great
    world . . .
What strength may we take from our Past, what promise
    hold for our Future?

And the one brother leaned and whispered:
"I put my strength in a book,
And in that book my love . . .
This, with my love, I give to America . . ."
And the other brother leaned and murmured:
"I put my strength in a life,
And in that life my love,
This, with my love, I give to America."

Lilacs bloom for Walt Whitman
And lilacs for Abraham Lincoln.

Then my heart sang out: This strength shall be our
    strength:
Yea, when the great hour comes, and the sleepers wake
    and are hurled back,
And creep down into themselves
There they shall find Walt Whitman
And there, Abraham Lincoln.

O Spring, go over this land with much singing
And open the lilacs everywhere,
Open them out with the old-time fragrance
Making a people remember that something has been
    forgotten,
Something is hidden deep—strange memories—strange
    memories—
Of him that brought a sprig of the purple cluster
To him that was mourned of all . . .
And so they are linked together
While yet America lives . . .

While yet America lives, my heart,
Lilacs shall bloom for Walt Whitman
And lilacs for Abraham Lincoln.

Stephen Vincent Benét
1898–1943
and
Rosemary Carr Benét
1898–1962

T HE Pulitzer Prize winning novelist and poet Stephen Vincent Benét was absorbed in the history of America. It was natural that among his largest enthusiasms would appear the figure of Abraham Lincoln. His reverence for Lincoln is most apparent in *John Brown's Body*, Benét's epic poem of the American Civil War, published in the fall of 1928. He had also written, apparently with much frustration, the script for Hollywood's 1930 movie version of Abraham Lincoln, in which the lead was taken by Walter Huston. And his enthusiasm is evident as well in the last things he did, for he had written in the final autumn of his life a radio script for Raymond Massey to use on Lincoln's birthday.

In a letter to his mother from Neuilly-sur-Seine on November 5, 1927, at which time he was at work on *John Brown's Body*, the poet spoke of Lincoln: "As for the politics of the time—well, I am a Union man or a Lincoln man. The more you read about him, the more genuine admiration for him you develop—perhaps that is one of the things that made me somewhat impatient with Phillips and Greeley and the rest of the rather loud-mouthed people who did their best to hinder him whenever they got a chance—oh, all with the finest and purest motives, but with so little sense or vision! Lee was a great man also but not likewise."

And then he speaks of a passage in *John Brown's Body:* "I am glad you liked the Lincoln thing—I think his soliloquy is fairly good—of course much of it is taken from his own words though not the dog idea. But I rather liked the conception of his telling God a story—he did it to everyone else whenever he was worried—and I think it is in his character."

With his wife, Rosemary, Benét began in May of 1933 the writing of A *Book of Americans.* The book was meant as a children's book, and when it appeared later that year with illustrations by Charles Child it included poetic sketches of such memorable figures of American history as Benjamin Franklin, Johnny Appleseed, Daniel Boone, and Clara Barton. Though most of the poems came easily we know that Benét worked hard on the Lincoln lyric, that he revised and rewrote. And Lincoln emerged as the "green pine" that "kept on growing."

ABRAHAM LINCOLN

1809–1865

Lincoln was a long man.
He liked out of doors.
He liked the wind blowing
And the talk in country stores.

He liked telling stories,
He liked telling jokes.

"Abe's quite a character,"
Said quite a lot of folks.

Lots of folks in Springfield
Saw him every day,
Walking down the street
In his gaunt, long way.

Shawl around his shoulders,
Letters in his hat.
"That's Abe Lincoln."
They thought no more than that.

Knew that he was honest,
Guessed that he was odd,
Knew he had a cross wife
Though she was a Todd.

Knew he had three little boys
Who liked to shout and play,
Knew he had a lot of debts
It took him years to pay.

Knew his clothes and knew his house.
"That's his office, here.
Blame good lawyer, on the whole,
Though he's sort of queer.

"Sure, he went to Congress, once,
But he didn't stay.
Can't expect us all to be
Smart as Henry Clay.

"Need a man for troubled times?
Well, I guess we do.
Wonder who we'll ever find?

Yes—I wonder who."

That is how they met and talked,
Knowing and unknowing.
Lincoln was the green pine.
Lincoln kept on growing.

Rosemary, too, contributed to the Lincolniana with a sketch of Lincoln's mother. "Nancy Hanks" was always a poem that Benét himself very much admired. It is made dramatic through the person of Nancy Hanks herself who inquires plaintively after her son, whose greatness she was never to know.

NANCY HANKS

1784–1818

If Nancy Hanks
Came back as a ghost,
Seeking news
Of what she loved most,
She'd ask first
"Where's my son?
What's happened to Abe?
What's he done?

"Poor little Abe,
Left all alone
Except for Tom,
Who's a rolling stone;
He was only nine
The year I died.
I remember still
How hard he cried.

"Scraping along
In a little shack,
With hardly a shirt
To cover his back,
And a prairie wind
To blow him down,
Or pinching times
If he went to town.

"You wouldn't know
About my son?
Did he grow tall?
Did he have fun?
Did he learn to read?
Did he get to town?
Do you know his name?
Did he get on?"

Lincoln occupies a large place in *John Brown's Body*, which Allen Tate insists is "the most ambitious poem ever undertaken by an American on an American theme," and the portrait provided is most sympathetic. We see him in his political associations, and in his domestic life. But for the most part he is the President, upon whose broad shoulders the burden of the war reposes. He is the Lincoln of the Capitol, sleeplessly watching and waiting, a gaunt and haggard man.

In Book Two of the poem the figure of the President is neatly sketched in. He is homely and awkward, but not without dignity. His virtues are honesty and self-confidence and kindness as "large and plain as a prairie wind." He feels uncomfortable in Cabinet meetings and he is plagued by office-seekers. He is tired, yet tolerant. With an unerring instinct he reads the characters of Seward and Chase. For him they are like two pumpkins in a sack—and how much easier to carry the two, which balance each other, than to jostle along with one. He reflects soberly on Jefferson Davis and on his own seemingly lesser qualifications, and then his mind turns to business, which means first the "calling of seventy-five thousand volunteers."

After the Battle of Bull Run we see the President in receipt of Horace Greeley's hysterical letter calling for an armistice. Lincoln is beleagured and confused by a thousand counsels, by "madness along the streets." But patiently, and true to his idea, he starts "kneading the stuff of the Union together again."

After Malvern Hill the President appears with a face "deeper furrowed than ever," but there "has been a growth in the man." Still at school to military tactics he yet has found the strength to decide unequivocally and to bear the burden of that decision. His are the hands that hold the reins over his horses, Halleck and McClellan.

In Book Five of the epic we see Lincoln as he sees himself, in a long soliloquy. It is two months after his writing of the Emancipation edict, and, having taken Seward's good advice, he is still waiting for a Union victory and a propitious moment for issuing formally the proclamation. It is September in Washington, September 17, 1862, and the President is found three miles out of the capital, under the tall trees which shade the Soldiers' Home, precisely where Walt Whitman so often observed him. He stares into the distant fog, waiting for news from Sharpsburg, where by now, as he supposes, General McClellan has engaged Lee.

In the course of his meditation Lincoln reflects on all he has been through, on all that has brought him to this pass. He speculates on God's will, and then turns to Him in prayer. It is here that he tells the little story of the hunting-dog, on which Benét remarked in his letter to his mother. From the anecdote he compares himself to that "old, deaf hunting-dog," whose only virtue was tenacity and whose only equipment was endurance, who though decrepit "once he gets his teeth in what he's after . . . don't let go until he knows he's dead."

The soliloquy is interrupted finally with news from Maryland. Impatiently the President seizes on the details. It is Antietam—and this, then, is the victory for which he has waited! And now, faithful to his promise, and with strength and hope restored, he announces, just five days after McClellan's "victory," that "on the 1st day of January, A.D. 1863, all persons held as slaves within any state or designated part of a state shall be then, thenceforward, and forever free."

But the war drags on. McClellan will not move, and impatiently Lincoln relieves him. Battles are won and lost, but Richmond seems far away, even in the fall of 1864. And now Lincoln is anxiously awaiting election returns and considering how best to assist the new President and his Cabinet to take Richmond and bring the long, long conflict to an end. But he is brought at last a different kind of news: first, that he has been reelected and is "sure of being President four years more"; and then, in the spring, on April 2, that Lee has abandoned Petersburg and Richmond.

With the war virtually over, the poet discovers Lincoln walking alone, unguarded, up and down through the streets. Somehow he wanders to General Pickett's house, speaks to his wife, introduces himself as "just one of George Pickett's old friends," and is stared after as he passes down the street past sordid and unhappy city scenes.

Finally Stephen Vincent Benét presents Abraham Lincoln on the day of the assassination. The President has wakened from a prophetic dream, which he has misinterpreted:

from
JOHN BROWN'S BODY

The gaunt man, Abraham Lincoln, woke one morning
From a new dream that yet was an old dream
For he had known it many times before
And, usually, its coming prophesied
Important news of some sort, good or bad,
Though mostly good as he remembered it.

He had been standing on the shadowy deck
Of a black formless boat that moved away
From a dim bank, into wide, gushing waters—
River or sea, but huge—and as he stood,
The boat rushed into darkness like an arrow,
Gathering speed—and as it rushed, he woke.

He found it odd enough to tell about
That day to various people, half in jest
And half in earnest—well, it passed the time
And nearly everyone had some pet quirk,
Knocking on wood or never spilling salt,
Ladders or broken mirrors or a Friday,
And so he thought he might be left his boat,
Especially now, when he could breathe awhile
With Lee surrendered and the war stamped out
And the long work of binding up the wounds
Not yet begun—although he had his plans
For that long healing, and would work them out
In spite of all the bitter-hearted fools
Who only thought of punishing the South
Now she was beaten.
                    But this boat of his.
He thought he had it.

"Johnston has surrendered.
It must be that, I guess—for that's about
The only news we're waiting still to hear."
He smiled a little, spoke of other things.

That afternoon he drove beside his wife
And talked with her about the days to come
With curious simplicity and peace.
Well, they were getting on, and when the end
Came to his term, he would not be distressed.
They would go back to Springfield, find a house,
Live peaceably and simply, see old friends,
Take a few cases every now and then.
Old Billy Herndon's kept the practice up,
I guess he'll sort of like to have me back.
We won't be skimped, we'll have enough to spend,
Enough to do—we'll have a quiet time,
A sort of Indian summer of our age.

He looked beyond the carriage, seeing it so,
Peace at the last, and rest.

They drove back to the White House, dressed and ate,
Went to the theatre in their flag-draped box.
The play was a good play, he liked the play,
Laughed at the jokes, laughed at the funny man
With the long, weeping whiskers.
                              The time passed.
The shot rang out. The crazy murderer
Leaped from the box, mouthed out his Latin phrase,
Brandished his foolish pistol and was gone.

Lincoln lay stricken in the flag-draped box.
Living but speechless. Now they lifted him
And bore him off. He lay some hours so.
Then the heart failed. The breath beat in the throat.
The black, formless vessel carried him away.

Charles Olson

1910–

AMONG the contemporary poets there continues an energetic interest in the Lincoln legend. One who has explored in the traditional way the myth-making possibilities of Lincoln, perhaps more impressively than any other poet of his time, is Charles Olson, the well-known Melville scholar.

A native New Englander, Olson is best known in his poetry for "The Kingfishers" and, more recently, for the *Maximus* poems. Much in the manner of one of his greatest admirers, William Carlos Williams, he has produced a significant number of beautiful and provocative lyrics. One of the most impressive of these is "Anecdotes of the Late War," which appears in *The Distances*, a collection of Olson's poems published in 1960. The poem might be regarded as a kind of *John Brown's Body* on a small scale; for, like Benét, Olson here examines the heroes and the dramatic moments of the Civil War.

Olson calls himself "an archeologist of morning," and that is precisely the role he plays for this poem. In an effort to get at the real significance of the war the speaker picks up from the battlefield a minie ball and contemplates it soberly. What was the Civil War?

> West Point it wasn't. Nor New England. Nor
> those cavalry
> flauntlets

As the Mexican War was
filibusterers
in the West,
and cadets
before Chapultepec: the elevator

goink down
from waterloo,
the Civil War

was the basement. Only nobody
except butternut
and his fellow on the other side
wanted to believe it . . .

To him an immense sense of tragedy lies in recognizing
that the great differences between the North and South are
imperceptible in the individuals who fought and died with
Grant and Stuart:

. . . that each one of them,

Butternut,

and Yankee Doodle,

weren't as different as North and South, farmer and fac-

tory, etc.

In the martyred Lincoln the will of a people to cohere, so
violated by the War Between the States, becomes across the
world the urgency of brotherhood:

And Lincoln

likewise (after Christ

Link-cone

Section 2 of the lyric refers us to the assassination and
shows us that in that incredible melodrama Abraham Lin-

coln took on once for all the immensities of myth and symbol, not only for the people of the nation whose union he had preserved, but for peoples the world over who feel the need for emancipation, spiritually, socially, politically. It is to his monument that the oppressed and underprivileged from all across the world come, hungry for freedom and dignity, in supplication and reverence.

from
ANECDOTES OF THE LATE WAR

that (like the man sd) Booth
killing Lincoln is the melodrama right with
the drama: Mister Christ and
Broadway

Or going out to Bull Run looking for
Waterloo. the
diorama. And having to get the fastidious hell home
that afternoon
as fast as the carriage horses
can't make it (Lee Highway
littered with broken
elegances

Reverse of
sic transit gloria, the
Latin American whom the cab driver told me
he picked up at Union Station had
one word of english—link-
cone. And drove him
straight to the monument, the man
went up the stairs and fell down on his knees
where he could see the statue and stayed there
in the attitude of prayer

Afterword

One hundred years following that black Good Friday the poets continue to draw upon the symbolic value of Lincoln. Some testify to his greatness as a man, or as President, associating him with Christ in his martyrdom; some look upon him as the figure in whom are most impressively and most completely exhibited the American ideals; some regard him as a supremely tragic human being, a Hamlet-type, caught up, as Delmore Schwartz puts it, "on History's ceaseless insane sums." For all of us, however, and the poets have recognized it best, the historical figure of Abraham Lincoln better than that of any other hero fills the need of a people to define in one name the promise of America.

ST. MARY'S COLLEGE OF MARYLAND LIBRARY
ST. MARY'S CITY, MARYLAND

THE LIBRARY
ST. MARY'S COLLEGE OF MARYLAND
ST. MARY'S CITY, MARYLAND 20686